'The voice of  *oh*

Matthew Jukes is the wine buyer at Bibendum restaurant and The Crescent wine bar, both on London's Fulham Road. He presented his own weekly radio feature on the BBC for five years, contributes to *Wine* magazine, writes a weekly column for the *Daily Mail* and is a regular guest on the BBC's prime-time Saturday night programme *Friends Like These*. He rides a Triumph Tiger.

PRAISE FOR MATTHEW JUKES'S *WINE*

First published in 2001 by
HEADLINE BOOK PUBLISHING

10 9 8 7 6 5 4 3 2 1

British Library Cataloguing in Publication Data
Jukes, Matthew
        The wine list 2002 : the top 250 wines of the year
        1. Wine and winemaking
        I. Title
        641.2'2

ISBN 0747244162

Printed and bound in Great Britain by Butler & Tanner Ltd, Frome and London.

Designed by Fiona Knowles, Pike Design

Headline Book Publishing
A division of Hodder Headline
338 Euston Road
London NW1 3BH

www.headline.co.uk
www.hodderheadline.com

THE WINE LIST 2002

MATTHEW JUKES
THE TOP 250 WINES OF THE YEAR

HEADLINE

To Isadora

CONTENTS

INTRODUCTION

The Wine List 2002 is the only book you'll ever need to track down the best wines in the world. With so much choice out there, I have endeavoured to take the risk factor out of buying wine by compiling a list of my favourite 250. I have also included the peripheral information you need in order to find these wines and decide what to serve with them. The only thing *you* have to sort out is who to open the bottle with.

I have split this pocket book into four main sections.

The Food and Wine section covers every corner of your fridge and pantry in a comprehensive A–Z of important cooking ingredients and favourite dishes. All you have to do is find the dish to then discover what style or styles of wine are best suited to bring out the flavours in the cooking without losing the intricacies of the wine and vice versa. This is the job that I do every week for the *Daily Mail's Weekend* magazine, and I have only been stumped once. (That dish is in this book, but you'll just have to read on to find out which recipe beat me.)

The Top 250 is the next section; and with 25,000 wines under my belt since I started working on this book just over a year ago, you could say that the maths has worked out very neatly indeed. Only one wine for every hundred samples tasted has made it into the Top 250. It has been a wildly varied marathon of flavours. It's always easy to chuck out the stinkers and, sadly, there are still millions of pounds worth of mediocre wine sold every year in the UK. There is little we can do about this other than vote with our palates and avoid buying poor wine. It has, however, been much tougher to whittle down the last five hundred or so.

The criteria needed to make it into the Top 250 are as follows. Aside from an epic taste that engenders all that is great about winemaking today, my chosen wines represent good value at whatever price point they hit. I have also only chosen wines that are ready to drink. It is pointless recommending a wine and then telling you to stick it in your cellar for a decade. So, a large number of these wines are fruit-driven, early-drinking styles and for that reason the New World, with its more generous, warm-weather flavours, has done well, with just over half of the 250 slots. The chosen 250 are also in pretty plentiful supply. I have warned each listed retailer and agent that there may be a stampede for these wines and they have ensured me that there is a hefty stock of each wine in the country. For a few wines, I have noted the UK agent's telephone number as opposed to the retail stockist. This is where a wine is so new that at the time of going to press nobody other than me and a few insiders had had a go at it. So, by the time of publication, each agent will have secured some retail outlets and will be happy to pass the details on to you. I have also tried to give a fair indication of the recommended retail price for each bottle. The vintages for each wine have been checked and re-checked. None should run out – famous last words.

In the end, Australia did very well. France, Italy, New Zealand, South America and Spain also impressed. But who'd have thought that there would be two Canadian wines and even a Tunisian one? The big shocks, though, are the omissions. There are very few wines from Burgundy or Bordeaux. They are generally just too expensive and in short supply. But if you are keen on these and other Fine Wines, then use my directory to locate your nearest independent specialist and ask them to track down specific wines for you.

To augment my Top 250, the Gazetteer is a comprehensive list of the best wine estates in the world. This is the ultimate who's who of the wine world. Use this when you are shopping for a special bottle or if you are in a restaurant with an unfamiliar wine list. You can even take this book abroad and look up the best wine producers in the country you are visiting. (Unless you're off to Iceland, Madagascar, Thailand and I'm sure a few others!)

The Directory is a list of the best independent wine merchants in the UK, plus their home town or postcode, and telephone number. I have included the hot-lines for each of the major supermarket chains and wine specialist chainstores. This is the best way to order and check stock for any wine you are after. This list is gold dust for wine enthusiasts.

Over the last year I have met thousands of people, from all corners of the wine world. I would like to thank you all for your time, energy, enthusiasm and wine. There are too many winemakers, agents, merchants, buyers and PRs to name individually, but without you The Wine List 2002 would not exist. I have enjoyed whittling down the world's cellar to a mere 250 bottles and I look forward to doing it all again next year. Special thanks must go to my wife Nathalie and my Ma and Pa. They are the most solid support team imaginable. Also, my close friends are to be congratulated for not being too cruel and inviting me out all the time, knowing I was chained to either the spittoon or my PC. Finally, thanks to my brilliant agent Robert Kirby at PFD and the army of talented staff at Headline, in particular, my delightful editor, Jo Roberts-Miller, for transforming innumerable floppy discs into a very smart book indeed. I owe you all a glass of wine, but how on earth does one decide what to buy these days…?

A-Z OF FOOD AND WINE COMBINATIONS

'Elvis Presley's dead, but there's poached eggs and red Burgundy down in the kitchen'

Peter Lofthouse, a friend

(While preparing breakfast, Peter heard a news bulletin on the radio and decided to uncork something to lift his flatmate's spirits.)

There are some wonderful combinations of food and wine that really set the flavours singing, but it is totally up to you what you want to drink with your dinner. So, in order to find the style of wine to match your food, search, in my list below, for an ingredient or a specific dish and you will find a wine, or style of wine, that should work well. Some wines are multipurpose – Sauvignon Blanc is everywhere, as is New World Merlot, so you should keep a few bottles of each at home, in readiness for unexpected guests or impromptu cooking. Even Beaujolais, one of the most derided styles of wine, is incredibly versatile – it pops up over 20 times in this section! So perhaps you'll have to reacquaint yourself with this underrated region.

When matching wine to food, the trick is to imagine the dish and think of its dominant flavours. A strongly flavoured dish will need an assertive wine while, conversely, mild, delicately flavoured food could do with a lighter style. There are no completely wrong combinations. Because, if you like it, then I'm not going to argue, as it is a matter of personal taste. What's more, there are some awesome and unlikely combinations that work well; crispy aromatic duck with Zinfandel, for example, or Christmas dinner with sparkling Shiraz. Another point to remember – are you serving any side dishes? And do they have any particularly strong tastes? Finally, consider how your dish is cooked. If the main ingredient is poached or steamed it will not pick up any extra cooking flavours on the way. If, however, the dish is fried, stewed, grilled or roasted, you would expect a stronger, more varied taste; poached salmon tastes distinctly different to seared, roast beef different to barbecued, and so on.

Once you have found your dish and a suitable style of wine, look in the gazetteer to locate the best producers of this wine. Also look in my Top 250 to find a bottle you can buy in the shops.

Vegetarian and vegan-friendly wines are often labelled as such these days. So ask if you are unsure, or look at the back labels on the bottles.

Two examples of how to use this guide:–
Asparagus and goat's cheese tart does not appear as a heading. So, check out both the 'Asparagus' and the two 'Cheese' headings. You will see that Sauvignon Blanc appears in each, so that would be the grape variety to go for. Whether you decide on a Sancerre or other Loire Sauvignon Blanc, or a New Zealand or New World Sauvignon is entirely up to you.

If you're out with your pals for a pub lunch, try ordering a bottle of Chilean Merlot and then work backwards to all of the dishes this wine adores. Your list could include: a cheese burger, Cheddar ploughman's, moussaka, smoked ham baguette, bangers and mash, pizza, macaroni cheese, lamb chops, enchiladas, shepherd's pie and many other dishes.

APÉRITIF WINE STYLES

To accompany *dry roasted almonds, cashews, canapés, crostini, crudités, gougères (cheese puffs), olives* and other pre-dinner nibbles: Champagne would be ideal if you're feeling flush, if not, then sparkling wines from Limoux, New Zealand, Australia or California would be just fine. Prosecco from Veneto in northern Italy is inexpensive, dry and superbly refreshing. Fino or manzanilla sherries are wonderful palate cleansers and although out of fashion somewhat, will certainly provoke conversation – who knows, you may even be considered ahead of your time. The least expensive (and often safest) option is an uplifting, cleansing, zingy dry white wine. There are thousands of these around. Make sure you go for unoaked styles and keep the price down so that you can step up a grade with the next bottle when the food hits the table. A neutral dry white can always be pepped up with a dash of Crème de Cassis to make a Kir (use dry sparkling wine or inexpensive Champagne to make a luxurious Kir Royale).

STARTERS AND MAIN COURSES

Anchovies Strongly flavoured and tangy, fresh or cured anchovies love dry, unoaked whites or juicy, dry rosés. Try Italy, Spain or France and keep to a low budget. Dry sherry is also a winner.

Antipasti The classic Italian mixture of artichokes, proscuitto, bruschetta, olives, marinated peppers and aubergines enjoys being twinned with light Italian reds like Valpolicella and

Bardolino, or clean, vibrant whites like Pinot Grigio, Orvieto, Verdicchio or Pinot Bianco.

Artichokes Bone-dry, unoaked whites are the order of the day, especially if you are dipping them in *vinaigrette* (see 'Vinaigrette'). Alsatian Pinot Blanc, Loire Sauvignon Blanc or Aligoté from Burgundy are perfect partners.

Asparagus Because of its own asparagussy characteristics, Sauvignon Blanc is the top match here. Australian or New Zealand versions have tons of flavour and would be better suited to asparagus dishes that have *hollandaise, balsamic vinegar* or *olive oil* and *Parmesan*. Loire Sauvignon Blanc and Chenin Blanc are great if the dish is plainer. Northern Italian whites, like Pinot Bianco or Pinot Grigio, as well as South African Sauvignon Blanc (in between New Zealand and Loire in style) would all do the job well.

Aubergines These sleek, black beauties are often used within recipes (*ratatouille*) rather than as a stand-alone item. If cheese or meat (*moussaka*) is involved their flavours take over from the aubergines, so light, youthful reds are generally required. Italian, southern French or Chilean Merlot are all good, just make sure they are not too heavy. If the dish is spicier or the aubergines are *stuffed*, you will need a more feisty red, but don't get tempted to buy anything too big (avoid Cabernet, Zinfandel, Shiraz etc). *Imam bayildi*, the classic aubergine, onion, olive oil and tomato dish is a winner with juicy, chilled Chilean Merlot, bright purple Valpolicella, glossy Sardinian Cannonau or Montepulciano d'Abruzzo.

Avocado If undressed, put some clothes on then start cooking. If the avocado is *undressed*, you need light, unoaked whites, in particular Sauvignon Blanc, Muscadet or Bourgogne Aligoté. If *dressed* with vinaigrette or with Marie Rose sauce for a prawn cocktail, richer Sauvignon Blancs, even with a touch of oak, are fine, as are white Rhônes and Alsace Pinot Blanc.

Bacon This usually pops up as an ingredient in a dish and not as the sole item, however if you feel like a wine to accompany a *full English breakfast* with black pudding then chilled red Côtes-du-Rhône or Beaujolais would be superb. If, however, you are using grilled *pancetta* or *lardons* in a salad, remember that the salty flavour and/or the smoked taste could encourage you to move away from a white wine to a juicy, fresh red. *Bacon and eggs* with red Burgundy is heavenly, if a bit decadent.

Barbecues The carefree, often haphazard, nature of barbecues, combined with the marinades and sauces, ensure an informal and flavour-packed occasion. New World gluggers, white or red, are the call, so long as they are assertive and juicy. Lightly oaked Chardonnay or Sémillon for whites, or Zinfandel, Merlot, Carmenère, Cabernet Sauvignon or Shiraz for reds, would all be a treat. Try Chile, Argentina, Australia, South Africa or New Zealand for likely candidates.

Beans With *baked beans* the tomato sauce takes over and you simply need fruit-driven reds to go with the tomatoey flavour. Any reds with fresh acidity such as those from the Loire, Spain or Italy should work, just try to keep the price down. Anything goes with *green beans* as they are hardly robust vegetables and you'd have to tiptoe with a fairy light white to let a green bean express itself. A *Tuscan bean salad* would demand a chilled light red or a tart, zingy white. If you have beans in a stew, such as *cassoulet* or some Spanish dishes, then Grenache-dominant wines, either from the south of France (Fitou, Corbières, Faugères or Minervois) or Garnacha-based wines from Spain (Navarra, Terra Alta, Priorato or Tarragona) would deal easily with the beanie ballast. *Black bean sauce* requires a radical rethink. Any wines subjected to this sweetness and intensity of flavour have to be huge, red and very smooth – Zinfandel is the only one with its hand up! *Refried beans*, either in tacos or other Mexican dishes, have a certain sludginess and earthy character that needs either rich whites, like New World Chardonnay (Chile and Australia do the best value), or fresh, fruity reds. I would try Bonarda, Sangiovese or Tempranillo from Argentina as a starting point, then head to Chile if you have no joy.

Beef There are so many beefy incarnations that the general rule must be that reds are the order of the day, but it is the size and shape of them that determines just how good the match will be. I could write an entire beef and wine chapter, but I'll endeavour to be *boeuf* and get to *à point*. *Roast* (or *en croûte/Beef Wellington*) Sunday lunches lend themselves to a degree of formality, perhaps even a modicum of decorum, and when you all gather around the table you are at liberty to push the boat out. It is at times like these when old-fashioned gentleman's claret really makes sense. Don't ask me why, but fine wines such as claret (red Bordeaux), Bandol, northern Rhônes – Hermitage, Cornas or Côte-Rôtie – or even Italy's answer to an Aston Martin, the Super-Tuscans, are simply magnificent with this king of beef dishes. Now not one of these wines is cheap. Nowhere near, in fact, so I would also recommend top Australian Cabernets from Margaret River (Western Australia) or indeed Californian Cabernets from the Napa Valley. Again fairly dear, they will give the richness and complexity that your palate is yearning for. However, if you are on a budget, try to replicate the flavours of the aforementioned great wines by clever selection. Not all of Bordeaux sub-regions are exorbitantly priced. The Côtes de Castillon, Bourg, Blaye and Francs, in a good year, can really hit the spot while Bergerac, Bordeaux's neighbour, or Languedoc reds (copying the Rhône model) would do very well. Most New World Cabernets around the tenner mark exhibit a degree of character and excitement that the sub-fiver wines inevitably lack.

Remember, if you like your beef 'rare', you can choose a younger, more tannic wine, as harsh tannins melt away with juicy, rare beef. But if you like your beef 'well done' then you will prefer an older wine, smoother and more harmonious, at its peak of drinking. *Stews, casseroles* and *pies* require heavier, structured reds, particularly if there is a meaty, rich gravy involved. Cabernet Sauvignon, Syrah (Shiraz), Piedmontese (northern Italian) reds, Zinfandel and Malbec are but a few of the grapes to go for. Track down wines from South Africa, Australia, California and Argentina. Southern Rhônes like Gigondas, Cairanne or Vacqueyras will be superb, as will Provençal or Languedoc reds made from the same grapes. Portuguese wines are worth considering with rich beef dishes, as the red wines from Dão and the Douro Valley are woefully underpriced and very impressive. The great, black wine from Cahors in southwest France also deserves a mention. *Boeuf bourguignon*, as the name suggests, usually enlists the help of a red Burgundy. But don't cook with anything expensive. Save your

food and wine

money for the 'drinking' wine and try to choose a better version of the one you have used to cook with. *Steak and kidney pie* needs earthy, rustic reds to match up to the gravy and the sturdy kidneys; Madiran and Cahors from France, Malbec from Argentina and New World war-horses like South African Pinotage enjoy this challenge. *Cottage pie*, with carrot, celery, onions and minced beef rarely requires anything more than a feisty, cheap red. Try Bulgaria, Hungary or southern Italy and wallow (go mad, buy two bottles). *Beef stroganoff* also demands rusticity, so search for southern Rhônes (Vacqueyras, Lirac, Cairanne or Gigondas); even Côtes-du-Rhône from the right domaines can be a joy. *Hungarian goulash* would be all the more authentic if a Hungarian red wine joined it. Good luck. I have yet to find the dream date, so head straight for Chilean Cabernet or Carmenère. *Steak* is a more direct flavour than a stew, so less brutish, finer wines can be dragged out of the cellar (or shop). Try Chianti, Brunello di Montalcino, Ribera del Duero, Californian Merlot, top end Cru Beaujolais, Crozes-Hermitage, St-Joseph, South African, Argentinian and New Zealand Cabernet Sauvignon, and all other classy reds. With *steak au poivre*, the pungent, ground peppercorns take over each mouthful, so look for meaty (peppery) wines like the northern Rhône reds or their cousins from further afield – Shiraz from Australia or South Africa, or South African Pinotage. *Burgers*, one of my all time favourite dishes (at home!), often served with ketchup, cheese or relish, need fruit-driven, less expensive reds like Italian Dolcetto, Spanish Garnacha, young Rioja Crianza, Californian Zinfandel, Chilean or South African Merlot, and again the ever versatile, meaty South African Pinotage. *Chili con carne* is a funny dish to match wine to but again, as with burgers, you are searching for fruitier styles like Aussie Merlot. *Steak tartare* is another weird dish to match wine to but works terrifically well with light reds and rosés. Tavel rosé and other Grenache-based rosés are perfect, as are Pinot Noirs like Sancerre red or rosé. If you fancy splashing out, then rosé Champagne is the ultimate combo, but go easy on the capers, if served. *Cold, rare roast beef salad* and other cold beef dishes need fresh reds with low tannins – Beaujolais, Valpolicella, red Loires (either Cabernet Franc or Gamay) or Argentinian Bonarda would work. The only occasion you can break the red-wine-with-beef rule (there has to be one) is with *carpaccio* (raw/rare) or *bresaola* (air-dried); the wafer-thin sliced beef dishes can handle whites. Any dry Italian white or light Montepulciano-style red would be good. Just stay away from big reds and whites.

Capers Sauvignon Blanc is the best match here, as it can cut through the peculiar tanginess experienced when you munch on a caper. Other than Sauvignon, stick to dry, fresh whites.

Caviar Ridiculously decadent, but if you can afford caviar, you will no doubt be able to buy Champagne. If there is caviar in a sauce then consider the main ingredients in the dish. Sauvignon Blanc is always a safe bet, but poached sea bass (for example) with a Champagne and caviar sauce would, bankrupt you for a start, and would follow the sea bass more than the caviar in the wine-matching process, so read on for the 'Fish' section.

Charcuterie A selection of charcuterie (or *assiette de charcuterie* including saucisson, salami, ham etc) often contains fairly diverse flavours along a similar textural theme. Assertive rosés, top quality Beaujolais or Loire Gamay would be my first choices. Light to medium Italian reds, like Valpolicella, Morellino di Scansano, Montepulciano d'Abruzzo or Sicilian Aglianico or Nero d'Avola would also be a good match. White wine lovers might prefer Riesling, which usually manages to harness at least as much flavour intensity as the reds anyway. Do watch out for pickles, gherkins/ cornichons or caperberries served alongside charcuterie, as vinegar is dangerous when it comes to wine. You'll not be able to taste the next mouthful! So tap the pickles first, to knock off as much vinegar as possible. (For *chorizo* and *spicy salami* see 'Pork'.)

Cheese (cooked) There is an entire 'cheese-board' section at the end, but here I will deal with cheese in cooking. *Cauliflower cheese* and *cheese sauces*, depending on the sort of cheese used, needs medium- to full-bodied whites such as New World Chardonnays or Sémillons. As for reds, fresh acidity and pure fruit lead us to wines from the Loire, or even to Chilean Carmenère or Merlot, Italian Dolcetto or Freisa or youthful Rioja or Navarra from Spain. *Fondue*, not my favourite form of food fun, needs bone-dry whites to cut through the waxy, molten cheese. If you were to be a perfectionist you would head in search of the innocuous wines from Savoie; Chignin-Bergeron, Abymes, Crépy or Apremont would be so exact you would probably be offered a job in the V&A for attention to detail. However, if you are simply after pleasant tasting wines, then well-balanced, fully ripe (as opposed to exasperatingly lean, teeth-strippingly acidic) styles like Alsatian Pinot Blanc, Riesling and Sylvaner, and Loire Sauvignon Blanc would be a joy. As would dry Portuguese white and even northern Italian numbers.

Raclette, the rather disappointingly one-dimensional fondue-and-potato-style dish, fancies light red Burgundies or Beaujolais. With *cheese soufflé*, one of the masterpieces of the cooked cheese repertoire, you can really go out on a limb. Argentinian Torrontés, or any aromatic, dry whites like dry Muscat (Alsace), Riesling (Aussie or Alsace) or even lighter Gewürztraminer (from anywhere decent) would be delicious. If the soufflé has any other hidden ingredients remember to consider them prior to plumping for a bottle. *Mozzarella*, with its unusual milky flavour and springy texture, is well suited to Italian Pinot Bianco, Pinot Grigio, Vernaccia, Gavi and Verdicchio. All Italians, but what do you expect, a revolution? *Grilled goat's cheese* is equally at home with Sancerre and all other Sauvignon Blanc wines. Lighter reds also work, particularly if you are tucking into a salad with ham on board as well. Goat's cheese is pretty versatile, just avoid oaked whites and heavy reds and consider the context in which it is being served.

Chicken Chicken loves whites and reds alike, but is a touch fussy when it comes to grape varieties. Chardonnay is its favourite white, with Riesling coming in second. Pinot Noir is chicken's favourite red, with Gamay a close second. This means that chicken loves every bit of my beloved Burgundy region, and who can blame it? Lighter dishes like *cold chicken* or *turkey* are fairly versatile, with picnic-style wines doing the job nicely. Try red Beaujolais and white Mâcon for really authentic harmony. *Cold chicken and ham pie* goes well with lighter red Rhônes, Beaujolais or Loire red and rosé. *Poached chicken* can handle the same sort of red wines, but perhaps those with a little more volume; Old or New World Pinot Noirs, for example. White wine companions include lighter New

World Chardonnay or French Country Viognier, giving delicious results. Possibly my favourite dish of all time, *roast chicken,* once again follows this theme a stage further. Finer red and white Burgundy, elegant Australian or Californian Chardonnay and Pinot Noir and top flight Beaujolais are required. *Coq au vin* also works well with red Burgundy, but you can scale the wine down to a Chalonnais, Bourgogne rouge (from one of my reputable producers, of course) or Hautes-Côtes level. *Chicken casserole* or *pot pie* ups the ante further, getting a broader brief to play with. Lighter Rhône reds and New World Grenache, as well as mildly oaky Chardonnays, are all in with a chance. *Chicken and mushroom pie, fricassée* and *creamy sauces* call out beyond Chardonnay to other varieties such as dry Riesling (from Alsace, Australia and New Zealand), Alsatian Tokay- Pinot Gris and Rhône whites. New World Pinot Noir (California and New Zealand) is the only token red variety to feel truly at home here. We now throw a few obstacles in front of the poor bird as *chicken Kiev* changes everything. Full, rich, even oaked Sauvignon Blanc is needed to take on the garlic – California does this well with Fumé Blanc.Not content with this hurdle, *coronation chicken,* depending on who is making it, can have a bit of a kick, so dry Riesling (from Clare Valley in Australia, or New Zealand) would be worth trying. Lastly, *barbecued chicken wings* can be nuclear-hot (my brother seems to be able to destroy an inordinate number of these) and in my experience beer is often the only saviour. If, for some reason, you are a mild-mannered person, who would like to spare the palates of your guests, then a regular, inexpensive New World Chardonnay with a touch of oak would be lovely. The only thing to watch out for with *turkey* is the cranberry sauce factor. Often a fresh, young

Rioja or New World Pinot Noir or Merlot complements this red fruit flavour well. At Christmas, Rioja again is a winner as the cocktail sausages, bacon and sprouts combo takes the flavour spotlight away from the turkey. If you are very brave (or totally ahead of your time), then a sparkling Shiraz from Australia would be fantastic and celebratory at the same time.

Chilli *Enchiladas*, *chimichangas*, *fajitas* and any other *Mexican dishes* as well as *chili con carne* and, of course, *diablo-style/dragon's breath pizzas*, are all enlivened with a liberal dose of chillies. You need thirst-quenching, chillable reds like Italian Primitivo or New World Merlot to cool you down and even your palate out. If you want to drink white wines then New World oaked Chardonnay, chilled, will have enough body to handle the heat.

Chinese The main problem when matching wine to Chinese food is that you invariably feel the need to have a spoonful of every dish on your plate, thus mixing flavours wildly. Sweet-and-sour crashes in on spicy, with plain, stir-fried food struggling for a break in the palate action. Chinese-friendly wines must be multi-skilled, fruit-driven wines with purity and fine acidity. Firmly tannic, youthful reds and oaky, full-bodied whites are out of bounds. White grape varieties to consider, in unoaked form, are Sauvignon Blanc, Riesling, Sémillon, Pinot Gris and Gewürztraminer. Reds are a little more difficult, as there are only a few truly juicy varieties, but New World Merlot and Zinfandel are usually safe bets. It is no surprise that New Zealand and Australian wines do well with this style of cooking, with Asia on their doorstep. *Crispy aromatic duck* is a dead-cert with chilled Chambourcin from Australia, or Californian Zinfandel.

Chutney see 'Pâté' and 'Pork'.

Duck *Roast* or *pan-fried* duck is generally served with fruit or fruity sauces. Therefore we need fruity wine as well. Reds are the order of the day with New World Pinot Noir, Beaujolais, Rioja, Italian Barbera, Australian Chambourcin and any other super-juicy, berry-drenched wine doing the job. *À l'orange* changes the colour of wine needed, but you still require full-flavoured, juicy wines. Alsace or Clare Valley Riesling, or Alsatian Tokay-Pinot Gris will have enough richness and oiliness to work. With *cherries*, mature Burgundian Pinot Noir, top notch Barbera from Piedmont, Reserva Rioja and medium-weight Zinfandels from California are all excellent. The more robust dish of *confit de canard* requires meatier reds with backbone and grip, like those from Bandol in Provence, Languedoc, Roussillon or from the southwest of France, for example Madiran, Cahors or Collioure.

Eggs For *quiche, soufflés* or *light savoury tarts* think of the main ingredient in them and consider its impact on the dish. Also, what are you eating alongside? Once you have narrowed these flavours down, unoaked or lightly oaked Chardonnay would be a fair starting point. If mushrooms are involved, then light reds enter the frame. *Omelettes* (*frittata* or *savoury pancakes*) follow much the same rules, however for *oeufs en meurette* (poached eggs in red wine with lardons) you definitely need a red wine such as Beaujolais or red Burgundy. For *fried eggs*, see 'Bacon' and for *poached eggs*, for example on a salad, again look at the other ingredients. If the salad includes stronger-flavoured elements, but you prefer not to have Beaujolais, then Alsatian Riesling is a winner. For *quails' eggs*, see 'Apéritif Wine Styles'. Finally, *eggs benedict* has a lot going on, from the muffin base, via the bacon or ham and ending with the hollandaise. Youthful Côtes-du-Rhône is a classic combination and is so delicious that your guests will inevitably ask you to make another round of eggs each, sorry!

Fish The flavour of fish depends not only on the sort of fish you are cooking, but also, crucially, on how it is cooked. The general rule is the milder the flavour, the lighter the white wine. The richer the flavour, the heavier the wine. Fish cooked in red wine is one of the exceptions to a white-dominated section, as a light red would be preferable to a stronger white. From Bianco de Custoza, Austrian Grüner Veltliner, Menetou-Salon (Loire), white Burgundy (Mâcon, Rully, Meursault and so on), Californian Chardonnay, Jurançon Sec, Australian Marsanne or Sémillon, any Riesling or Viognier, the opportunities are endless. Just remember that poaching and steaming are milder, non-taste-altering ways of cooking while grilling, searing, frying and roasting all impart distinctive nuances to the fish. Also consider what you cooked the fish with; remember to check through the ingredients for strong flavours, such as lemon, capers, herbs etc.

The finer the piece of fish, often the more money you are prepared to spend on the wine. *Dover sole, turbot* and *sea bass,* at the top of my wish list, are all pricey and white Burgundy would be a real treat. Failing that, for a tenner, you could pick up a top South African Chardonnay, Australian Sémillon, Adelaide Hills or Clare Valley Riesling or Chardonnay, Riesling from Alsace, Lugana or Gavi from Italy, dry white Graves (Bordeaux), white Rhône wines and Spanish Albariño to go with these fish. *Halibut,*

John Dory, *sea bream* and *brill* all enjoy these styles of wine too, while *monkfish* and *hake* can take slightly weightier white, or even fresh light red, such as Beaujolais. *Salmon* (*poached* and *grilled*) also likes Chardonnay, whether it is from the Old or New World. *Trout* again likes Riesling, but add Chablis to the list, as well as the unusually scented French Country wine, Jurançon Sec. *Fish cakes*, especially high salmon content ones, go wonderfully with dry Riesling or Sémillon, particularly if you are partial to a generous spoonful of tartare sauce. *Red mullet* has enough character to handle rosé wines, making a pink partnership between plate and glass. *Kedgeree* is more tricky as the smoked haddock, cayenne, parsley and egg may make you consider a red. But don't, as you need to slice through this dish with rapier-like acidity and I'm sure you know which white grape does this best – Sauvignon Blanc. While we are on the subject, Sauvignon is the grape to have with *fish 'n' chips* (*cod*, *haddock* or *plaice*) because of the batter and vinegar (go easy). *Fish pie* is another occasion for Sauvignon Blanc to shine. The poshest combo would be Pouilly-Fumé or Sancerre, but if you fancy a trip to the New World, then New Zealand has to be the starting point for fans of this grape. Chenin Blanc, Aligoté and unoaked Chardonnay also perform well. *Fish soups* and *stews* tend to need more weight in a wine, and one of the most accurate matches would be a white Rhône wine made from Marsanne and Roussanne, or Viognier. Aussie Marsanne or Pinot Gris would also be a great option. *Sardines* need acidity to cut through their oily flesh; once again Sauvignon Blanc is the winner, but Pinot Grigio, Albariño, Aligoté, Gavi from Italy and even light reds, like Gamay, would be smashing. *Seafood risotto* is a favourite of mine and dry Italian wines like decent Frascati, Vernaccia di San Gimignano, Verdicchio Classico and Sicilian Chardonnay, along with South African Sauvignon Blanc and Chenin Blanc make a rather delicious combination. Remember that Chilean Sauvignon is often cheaper than both South African and New Zealand versions, so if you are having a dinner party with a big risotto or fish pie then look here for a load of bottles. *Canned tuna*, and its finer, paler version, *albacore*, just need unoaked, dry white wine. Albacore, however, has a more delicate flavour than pink tuna so take care not to swamp it. The Italian duo, Bianco di Custoza and Soave, are particularly agreeable. For *salade niçoise*, see 'Salads'. *Fresh tuna*, seared and served rare, secretly likes juicy, fresh reds and rosés. *Brandade (salt cod)*, with its garlic and oil components, can stand up to whites with a little more poke. Albariño, from Galicia in Spain, is a perfect choice, however Penedès whites and even light rosés are all within its grasp. *Herring*, *kippers* and *rollmops* all have a more robust texture thanks to the curing process. Once again, dry whites and rosés work well, but steer clear of oaked whites, as the power of the wine will overshadow the subtleties of the fish. *Smoked eel* is often served with crème fraîche and cream and is a little problematic for wine, but look for Austrian Riesling or Grüner Veltliner, German Pinot Gris or dry Riesling, and almost any dry wine from Alsace, and they should step up to the mark with style. *Smoked salmon* is perfect with Gewürztraminer whether it is from Alsace, Chile, or anywhere come to think of it; just buy a dry wine, not an off-dry version. The scent and tropical nature of Gewürz works amazingly well but so does Viognier and even Canadian Pinot Blanc. Do not forget Champagne, particularly if you are serving blinis topped with smoked salmon and caviar.

Smoked trout or *mackerel pâté* is a challenge for wine – fishy, smoky and creamy in one dish. French Viognier, Clare Valley Sémillon, Adelaide Hills Sauvignon Blanc and Pinot Gris (all Aussies), Alsatian Riesling and Pinot Blanc are all perfect matches. Lastly, *curries* or *Asian* fish dishes often sport spices, ginger and chilli so it is back to our favourite white saviour grapes of all time that we turn in search of a solution. New World Sauvignon Blanc's supreme confidence and Aussie and New Zealand Riesling's natural skill make this tricky challenge a walk in the park.

Game All flighted game, including *pheasant*, *quail*, *guinea fowl*, *woodcock*, *teal*, *grouse*, *snipe*, *wild duck* and *partridge* adore Pinot Noir. So red Burgundy would always be my first choice, with California, New Zealand and Oregon somewhere in the pack behind the leader. The riper and longer the bird is hung, the more mature the wine required. But I have enjoyed red Bordeaux, Italian Super-Tuscan, northern Rhône, Spanish Ribera del Duero and many other top reds with this heady style of cuisine. *Hare* in jugged form often uses port and redcurrant jelly in the recipe, so a red wine is needed, and a big one at that. Piedmontese reds made from Nebbiolo would have the brawn, as would big Australian Shiraz, Zinfandel from California or South African Pinotage. One cheaper and worthy source is the Douro Valley in Portugal, which makes red wines alongside port – and not only would you have a beefy wine, but it would be in perfect synergy with the port used in the ingredients. *Rabbit*, as well as being a less athletic version of a hare, is also less pungent and has lighter-coloured flesh. This time big reds are needed but not quite as insanely powerful as those suggested for hare. Chianti, Vino Nobile di Montepulciano (both from Tuscany),

Bandol (from Provence), Lirac, Vacqueyras and Gigondas (from the southern Rhône), Argentinian Malbec, South African Shiraz and Chilean Cabernet blends would be spot on. *Wild boar* again favours rich, brooding red wines. Depending on the style of dish, you could choose any of the aforementioned gamey reds. But this time add the two most noble of Italian wines Brunello di Montalcino and Barolo. *Venison* again loves reds and any wine in this section would do including Australian Cabernet Sauvignon and some of the better New Zealand Hawke's Bay Cabernets. Finally, *game pie*, served cold, behaves like chicken and ham pie (see above). If served hot, then serve the wines suggested for steak and kidney pie (again, see above).

Garlic *Roast* garlic tends to walk all over fine wines, so if you are partial to shoving a few bulbs in the oven then keep the wine spend down and follow the main dish's lead. *Garlic prawns, mushrooms* and *snails* all need aromatic, bone-dry Sauvignon Blanc to save the day. *Aïoli* (garlic mayonnaise) can add excitement to chicken, potatoes, fish, soups and so on, but just watch out for it because you'll get a shock if your wine is not prepared. (*Chicken Kiev* appears in the chicken section.)

Goose The best wines for roast goose lie somewhere between those best suited to game and those best suited to chicken. This means that lighter red Burgundy and Pinot Noirs in general are the reds to choose, while big, rich Chardonnays and Rieslings make up the white team.

Greek See 'Mezze'.

Ham Beaujolais-Villages, Chilean Merlot, Crianza Navarra and Rioja and youthful South African Pinotage all provide the juiciness to complement a glorious ham. The golden rule is to avoid any reds that are too tannic or acidic – mellow styles are required. *Parma ham* (prosciutto) and melon, *jamón serrano* and *pata negra* like dry German Riesling, many of the aromatic Trentino and Alto Adige whites from northern Italy and mildly oaked Spanish Viura. *Honey-roast ham* needs mouth-filling, oily, dry whites like dry Muscat, Viognier, Riesling and Gewürztraminer. Search for these in Alsace, the Rhône Valley and French Country wines (and grab some *figs* to eat alongside while you are at it). *Ham hock* with lentils or boiled Jerseys, and beetroot or peas (my favourite combinations) is a treat with smart rosé, and there are some out there, so go for Tavel in the southern Rhône or Sancerre rosé. *Smoked ham* has a fairly strong aroma and flavour and Tokay-Pinot Gris from Alsace would be exact. If you favour red wine then choose a Merlot from Australia or Chile and chill it a degree or so to retain the freshness. *Gammon steak* (avoiding pineapple or peaches, please) makes a neat partnership with oily, unoaked whites. All Alsatian wines and most dry German Rieslings would be delicious, as would the world-class Rieslings from Australia's Clare Valley. Sémillon rarely gets the call up for a specific dish, but Aussie versions, and dry white Bordeaux (both with a smattering of oak) are stunning with gammon steak.

Indian Depending on the heat of the dish – nothing will get through a vindaloo! – rosé, Gewürztraminer, Riesling and Sauvignon Blanc all the way up to pretty hefty chilled reds will do. Think of the main themes of the dinner and go for a much juicier version than you would for a non-Indian dish.

Japanese *Sushi* is a strange one to drink wine with as surely tea or saké would be more appropriate? However, sparkling wines and Champagne are a treat with the best sushi, and the ever-ready Sauvignon Blanc is there as a stand-by. *Teriyaki* dishes are a nightmare to match, as the sweetness and fruitiness in the glossy soy and saké glaze is particularly dominant on the palate. Zinfandel from California, super-ripe Merlot from South Australia and Nero d'Avola from Sicily would manage this huge challenge. *Wasabi* is a wine assassin; Wasabi 1, Wine 0.

Kidneys Lambs' kidneys generally take up the flavour of whatever they are cooked in and mustard is often used, so keep the reds firm and characterful – Chianti, Barbera (both Italian), Rioja, Navarra (both Spanish), Languedoc and the Rhône Valley (both French) would all be worth consideration. (For *steak and kidney pie* see 'Beef'.)

Lamb Classically speaking there is nothing more accurate than red Bordeaux for *roast lamb* or *lamb chops*. However, reds from Bergerac and Burgundy, South Africa's Pinotage and Shiraz, California's Merlot, Australia's Shiraz and Cabernet blends, Spain's Rioja and Argentina and Chile's Cabernets and Merlots are all up with a shout. In fact, if you keep the wine neither lightweight nor heavyweight, but somewhere in the middle you will do well. You can, of course, go bonkers on the price of the wine or keep within a tighter budget; lamb is less critical than, say, beef or game. However, the way it is cooked should influence your final wine choice. If cooked pink, the range of suitable wines is enormous (any of the above). If well done, then a fruitier style of red should be served, so head to the

New World countries listed above. Watch out for the gravy and the mint sauce, as an abundance of either could trip the wine up. *Shepherd's pie* is an incredibly easy dish to match to red wine. In fact, just open what you feel like, it will probably be spot on. *Lamb pot roast* and *casserole* tend to be a little richer than a chop or roast lamb because of the gravy. Again, do not spend too much on the wine, as rustic Languedoc or southern Rhône red would be perfect. *Lamb shank* is another relatively easy dish to match to red wine, with European examples from Portugal, Spain, Italy and France all offering enough acidity and structure to cut through the juicy meat. *Moussaka*, with cheese, onion, oregano and aubergines all thrown into the mix, is altogether different. Lighter, fruit-driven reds such as New World Pinot Noir, Primitivo from southern Italy or reds from La Mancha in Spain should work well. *Stews* like *navarin* (with vegetables), *Irish stew*, *cassoulet* or *hot pot* all have broader shoulders when it comes to reds. Beefier southern French reds from Fitou, Corbières, Madiran, Faugères, Minervois or Collioure would be accurate. And from further afield, Malbec from Argentina or Carmenère from Chile, as well as lighter Aussie Shiraz, would suit these dishes down to the ground. *Cold lamb* follows the same rules as beef, and to a certain extent ham, in that fruity, light reds and juicy medium-weight whites can work well. Beaujolais is, again(!), a great partner for the occcasion, while Chardonnay in any of its following guises would enliven the dish – medium-priced white Burgundy, Chardonnay from Margaret River, Adelaide Hills or Yarra Valley (Australia) or Nelson or Marlborough (New Zealand); lighter South African and Chilean styles. Lastly, we come to *kebabs*, one of lamb's noblest incarnations. You would struggle to wrestle with a kebab and a glass of wine while walking down the street after a late night out. But on the off chance that you make it home before tucking in, then a glass of Aussie Chardonnay from one of the reliable brands would be useful thirst-quencher and not something you'd regret opening the next morning.

Liver *Calves' liver with sage*, yum. Here the main rule is to choose a red wine with firm acidity. Loire reds are the pick of the bunch; Saumur-Champigny, Chinon or Bourgueil are relatively inexpensive and a perfect match. Northern Italian reds like Valpolicella, Trentino Teroldego or Cabernet all have the required freshness and grip. *Liver and bacon* needs a touch more spice in a red wine, so move to a warmer part of France or Italy (i.e. head south); Bordeaux and Chianti will do.

Meat as in balls (see 'Pasta'), pies (see 'Beef'), loaf (see 'Terrines').

Mexican *Fajitas, enchiladas, tacos, burritos, salsa* and all things Mexican lead to beer. Beer has undeniable thirst-quenching properties, crucially needed for tangy, chilli-hot food. But if you fancy a glass of wine, you need juicy, chillable reds like Primitivo (from southern Italy), Merlot from Chile and Zinfandel from California to cool you down and smooth out the palate. As for whites, inexpensive New World oaked Chardonnay or Sémillon (or a blend of the two), chilled down ice-cold, will allow you to taste the food and the wine in turn, without suffering chilli overload.

Mezze (or **Meze**) This has got to be a chance for dry Greek whites to shine. There are enough out there to really hit the mark, but if you are unable to track a good one down, then try Muscat,

Pinot Blanc or Sylvaner from Alsace, New Zealand Sauvignon Blanc or Argentinian Torrontés. Also try to find dry Muscat from Australia, another rarity but stunning with mezze. Greek reds, to me, are lagging behind the whites in terms of quality. The cheapies are fine, but I would avoid spending more than £7 to £8, as you will be hard-pushed to justify it with so much competition out there; I'd rather look further afield, perhaps to Italy and Spain.

Mixed Grill Hurrah, real food! You must uncork a feisty southern Rhône red or its New World counterpart, a 'GSM' blend (Grenache, Shiraz and Mourvèdre), from Australia. Awesome.

Moroccan/North African Moroccan food differs in many ways to European dishes. But the most important factor when it comes to matching the food with wine is the particularly wide range of spices used and the outstanding aroma of each and every recipe. Counter this either with aromatic wines, or choose closed, neutral ones and let the food capture your senses. Spain, Italy and France are the first and obvious ports of call. And within these three great wine nations, my favourite aromatic white styles would be Albariño (from western Spain), Viognier (south of France) and Erbaluce (northwest Italy). Reds that work are Rioja (Spain), chilled Côtes-du-Rhône (France) and Nero d'Avola, Aglianico or Primitivo (southern Italy and Sicily). If you want to stay neutral, stick to Beaujolais or Pinot Blanc from Alsace. If you want to stray further from the Med, then choose Sauvignon Blanc from Stellenbosch (South Africa) for its herbal, lime juice character and Barossa Valley Bush Vine Grenache (South Australia) for its pure red berry fruit and herbal nose.

Mushrooms I am a wholehearted, unapologetic carnivore, but I can happily cook an evening's dinner oblivious of the fact that I have forgotten to include any 'meat' if mushrooms play a central role in my dish. It is strange, but I try to feel cheated while doing the washing up, but my body and palate are replete, so, hey, what's the problem? Clearly, veggies live a life of abstinence from many of the headings in this chapter, but can still experience 'meaty' food in terms of intensity and flavour when mushrooms (and other things) are wielded correctly. So, when matching wine to mushrooms, ignore the fact that they are fungi and imagine what task they are fulfilling in the dish. *Baked* or *grilled* mushrooms usually retain their essence and flavour, and cellar temperature reds (chilled a touch) should let the dish express itself. Make sure that you choose loose, open reds that are ready to drink, but that are not too dominant. *Creamy sauces* are always tricky; if you overdo the cream a robust, oaked Chardonnay or Sémillon is needed but if the cream features only in a supporting, swirly role, then refreshing reds like Merlot and Barbera would be superb. *Mushroom omelettes* are a classic example of how a mushroom can hold its own in an eggy, creamy arena. *Wild mushrooms* can be intensely gamey and foresty so aim for my 'Game' section and trade down in weight (and price). *Mushrooms on toast* are coming back in as a *de rigueur* starter – good news, as there is nothing that sets the palate up more for a main (wintry/meaty) course as perfectly executed mushrooms on toast. Wine-wise, look to the main course and downsize the style a touch, leaving something bigger in reserve for the main dish. If you are having a double serving, as a stand-alone, in-front-of-the-telly dinner, then try the fabulous Barbera and Dolcetto from northern Italy. These two varieties are becoming more widely available and don't half kick this dish into the goal. *Stuffed mushrooms* depend on what they are stuffed with. I know it is obvious, but cheesy, veggie ones work well with light reds. Lose the cheese, though, and rich whites are in with a shout; medium-sized Chardonnays and Rieslings are ideal. For *mushroom risotto* see 'Risotto'. For *mushroom tart*, see 'Eggs'.

Mustard Turn up the volume on the wine that you are drinking, whether white or red, if you have a mustard sauce, dressing or accompanying dish with a mustard theme. You do not need to go crazy, but a notch up on quality (a pound or two more in a similar-styled wine will do).

Olives see 'Apéritif Wine Styles', if you are nibbling them. But if cooking with them, in a lamb dish for example, take care not to introduce too much of the liquor from the tin as the water, brine or oil is pungent and can cast too strong an influence over the final taste of the dish. This will, in turn, affect the wine's chances of survival. The usual rule is to look at the main ingredient in the recipe and make sure that your chosen wine can be enjoyed alongside an olive, prior to its involvement in the dish. *Tapenade* is a funny old thing. Vehemently unfriendly when it comes to wine (unless you love dry sherry) it is best to go for bone-dry whites from cooler-climate regions, for example Frascati, Soave, Lugana and Vernaccia (all Italian), or Sauvignon de Touraine, Bergerac Sec, Jurançon Sec or Pacherenc de Vic Bihl from France.

Onion As a stand-alone dish, onion is at its best in *onion tart* and Alsatian Riesling is the only wine to drink alongside this noble offering. If you stray from this advice, I am certain you will receive a knock at the door from the wine police. If you conform, you will be in no doubt about the virtues of food and wine matching. Yes, this is a sermon. You may also see *caramelised* onions offered as a side dish, if so tread carefully. The intense sweetness, albeit tempered by the rest of your plate of food, can put a wine off. So eat and sip carefully – I chickened out of this one!

Oysters see 'Seafood'.

Paella Not worthy of a listing really, except that it is a mix up of ingredients and often crops up in 'what do I drink with...' questions. The answer is chilled Cabernet Franc (red Loire), Albariño (Spanish white) or French or Spanish Grenache-based rosés. Delish.

Pasta In the greater scheme of things, pasta virtually tastes neutral. But it is never served on its own! So, the trick is to consider what you are serving over, under or around it. Stuffed styles like *cannelloni, agnolotti, cappelletti, tortellini* or *ravioli* can contain veg, cheese, meat and all sorts, so bear this in mind. *Spinach and ricotta tortellini* soaks up juicy Italian reds like Barbera, from Piedmont, young, simple Chianti, Franciacorta, Bardolino and Valpolicella. *Seafood* pasta dishes, including *vongole* (clams), love serious Sauvignon Blanc, decent Frascati (over £5), Soave (again, break over the fiver barrier, for quality), Lugana and Vernaccia di San Gimignano. *Meatballs, spaghetti bolognese, lasagne,* and *meaty sauces* all respond to universal red wines. Keep the budget down and head for expressive, juicy examples that work in tandem with the dish as opposed to trying to score points. Consider all of Italy, many New World regions, except for hugely alcoholic wines, and, although heretical, anything bright and juicy from Spain. *Roasted vegetables* often pop up in pasta dishes allowing you to choose between richer whites and lighter reds. Not only is this an attractive veg-friendly dish, it also suits all wine palates (a safety dinner party dish for first-time guests). *Pesto* is a classic pasta combo, but on the face of it is remarkably hostile on the wine front. Oil, pine nuts, Parmesan and basil seem innocent enough, but combine them and you are snookered into dry whites, for safety. Go to Italian regions Friuli and the Alto Adige as your guide, and find any bone-dry whites. They grow Sauvignon Blanc up there, so at least you can rely on that stalwart grape, but otherwise Pinot Grigio, Tocai Friulano and Pinot Bianco would sort it out. *Red pesto* is a different call. Here go for light red wines and keep the temperature down to focus their fruit flavours. *Cheesy* and *creamy sauces* tend to be more dominant than the ingredients bound therein, so once again Bardolino, Dolcetto and Barbera from Piedmont, Montepulciano from Marche and medium-weight Chianti are sublime. If, for some reason, you want to stray from the hallowed shores of Italy in search of wine with pasta then there is even more choice. Medium-weight reds and dry whites are abundant, so go for it but just remember not to overshadow the dishes, particularly with higher-alcohol New World reds. For *tomato sauce*, see 'Tomato'. For *mushroom sauces*, see 'Mushrooms'.

Pâté Confusingly, pâté, regardless of its ingredients, is keen on white wines. The only reds that work are featherweights (like Beaujolais etc). In the white world, you need fruity, aromatic grapes from any decent wine-making country, but they must have a degree of sweetness, all of the way from technically dry (but still fruity – Riesling, Gewürztraminer and so on) up to genuine sweet wines. Pâté is usually served as a starter and so pouring a sweet wine can seem a little about face. But if you are serving pudding or cheese then you can happily open a bottle of sweet wine, serve a few small glasses for starters and finish it off during cheese or pud. Many sweet wines are sold in half bottles, so if it's a small gathering, you'll waste not a drop.

Chicken liver pâté is a standard that favours dry to medium German Riesling, Alsace Riesling or Pinot Blanc, or slightly sweet white Bordeaux. *Country pâté* is a catch-all term that often hints at a coarser texture of pâté of indeterminate origin. The safest bet here is again a light white. If you are pushed into a short wine list or a sparsely stocked off-licence, then play safe and buy dry whites, and hope for the best. If you have the luxury of choice then Alsace is a great start, with Riesling and Tokay-Pinot Gris being the plum choices. Head to the New World and you'll find Riesling in abundance in South Australia, while Chilean Gewürztraminer seems to be doing well, too. *Duck pâté* is fine, but *foie gras* (goose liver) is the real thing. We are now firmly in sweet wine territory. Sauternes, Loire and Alsace sweeties, Aussie botrytised Sémillon and with a tighter budget on the go, Monbazillac, Ste-Croix du Mont, Loupiac, Cadillac and Saussignac, Sauternes' taste-alike neighbours, all perform admirably. *Parfait*, the smoother, creamier version of pâté, tends to reveal its brandy ingredient more than a coarse pâté, so make sure your sweet wine is rich enough to cope with this. If you don't want to try a sweet wine, then 'nearly-sweet' or rich whites from Alsace work. 'Vendange Tardive' (late-picked) wines can have richness without cloying sweetness and will appease the non-sweet wine fans. Grapes to consider are Tokay-Pinot Gris, Gewürztraminer and

Riesling. *Smoked salmon pâté* and other fishy incarnations are well served by aromatic whites (see 'Fish'). One thing to remember with pâté dishes is that occasionally cheeky *chutney* (or *onion confit*) is served alongside, giving a fruit or veg explosion of flavour that, while enlivening the pâté itself, may confuse the wine. Not so Alsatian Vendange Tardive wines, mentioned above, whose spice and richness of fruit will love the added flavours. Drier wines will, however, suffer. I have already talked about gherkins and the like in my 'Charcuterie' section, so keep them under control as well.

Peppers *Raw peppers* crackle with freshness, crunchiness and zingy, juicy, healthy flavours. It is no surprise that Sauvignon Blanc (from almost anywhere) is the best grape for salads and raw peppers, as 'capsicum' is a classic tasting note for this variety. It is a marriage made in heaven, but if you want to try something different, then dry Chenin Blanc from South Africa or Italian Pinot Grigio would be splendid. *Piedmontese peppers* are a favourite Saturday lunch dish of mine, and with the olive oil, garlic and tomato, dry whites are required, especially if the traditional anchovy fillets are added on top. Assertive Sauvignon Blanc is the best option, although Verdicchio, Orvieto and Gavi (or less expensive Cortese-based whites) from Piedmont itself would be appropriate. A *stuffed pepper* depends more on the stuffing than on the pepper itself, so look to the filling for guidance. Generally speaking, meat or cheese stuffings go well with light Italian reds. *Marinated in olive oil*, peppers love any dry white wines; for consummate accuracy Italian is best, so find some Soave, Frascati or Friuli single varietals such as Pinot Grigio, Pinot Bianco, Traminer or Sauvignon Blanc.

Pigeon see 'Game', but cheaper!

Pizza Heroic pizzas rarely allow white wines enough space to be heard. However I suppose a wimpy vegetable or seafood pizza would need a white. Assuming you have a tomato base and cheese on top, the real point of a pizza is the richly flavoured unlimited number of palate-expanding toppings that you sling aloft; mushroom, onion, anchovy, caper, olive, beef, ham egg, pepperoni and, crucially, chillies. A real man's pizza has these and more, so you will have to find a feisty red and chill it down. My all-Italian pizza wine line-up includes: whites – Arneis, Soave, Bianco di Custoza, Verdicchio, Pinot Bianco, Pinot Grigio and Orvieto; chillable reds – Sardinian Cannonau, Freisa, Barbera and Dolcetto from Piedmont, Marzemino and Teroldego from Trentino, Bardolino and Valpolicella from Veneto and Montepulciano d'Abruzzo, Sangiovese di Romagna, Primitivo and Aglianico from further south.

Pork Pork pops up in many different incarnations. I have given the noble *sausage* its own section. And, no doubt, *pâté* and *terrine* lovers are happy that these two dishes also warrant a separate heading. I have also dealt with *charcuterie, cassoulet, bacon, full English breakfast* and *ham* in other sections. This pork heading endeavours to cover any other dishes not previously mentioned. So, first up the princely *pork pie* and its less exciting cousin the *Scotch egg*. A good pork pie is a real treat and while I'm sure that a pint of bitter is more than likely the ideal partner, a glass of red Cru Beaujolais or white Bourgogne Aligoté wouldn't go amiss. The Scotch egg somehow crops up in pubs and picnic, more than at the dinner table, and real ale is the preferred drink of choice.

But you won't put a foot wrong by ordering a juicy red wine either. I'm not sure about the hybrid pies with pickle or cheese (?) on the inside, but if you like a dollop of Branston or Piccalilli on the plate with your pie, then be ready for the wine to be sent into a spin. *Chorizo* and *salami* fall into the aforementioned 'Charcuterie' section, however remember that the spicier the salami, the cooler the red wine. A plate of chorizo is excellent with dry, clean sherry – manzanilla and fino are best. Next on the agenda, *spare ribs*, whether they are drenched in barbecue sauce or not, are prehistoric fare, so cave-man reds are needed to slake your thirst. Fruit, juice and texture are all essential ingredients, so we must head off to the New World in search of Argentinian Sangiovese, Bonarda or Tempranillo, Chilean Carmenère or Australian Shiraz. Californian Zinfandel and Cabernet would also work well, although expensively. *Rillettes*, (which can also be made of duck or rabbit) is one of pork's lighter sides. The fondanty, savoury, meaty dish, often served with a plate of cold meats, is white-wine friendly. Pinot Blanc, Sylvaner and Riesling from Alsace all work well. I have left the big daddy to last, *roast pork*. The number of ways to roast pork means that there is a pretty open brief when it comes to matching it to wine. One thing is certain – if you are going to serve a red, make it light. Pork is far more excited to be associated with white wine, though, particularly if there is apple sauce in a sauceboat moored alongside. Classy, unoaked Chardonnay from Chablis or Burgundy would be exact, although New World Chardonnays can hack it as long as they are not too rich and oaky. Riesling (dry and luxurious), Condrieu (super-dear northern Rhône frenzy), Vouvray (make sure it says 'sec' – dry – on the label), southern Rhône whites (thin on the ground but a lot of bang for your buck) are all worth a sniff.

Quiche (and posh tarts?) see 'Eggs'.

Rabbit see 'Game' apart from *rillettes* which love a little more scent and exotic nature than pork rillettes, so Marsanne, Roussanne and Viognier from anywhere in the world (Rhône is your starting point) or Pinot Blanc and Riesling (the richer styles from Alsace) would be mouth-wateringly spot on.

Risotto Generally the richness and texture of a risotto needs to be 'cut' with the acidity of a clean, dry white wine, with good fruit and flavour. But what have you got in your risotto? Bear the magic ingredient(s) in mind when matching wine to the creamy, cheesy (if you whack in a spot of Parmesan and butter alongside the stock) rice. Reds can work with *wild mushrooms*, but usually whites are better. *A la Milanese*, with saffron, can force a light, dry white into submission unless it has enough fruit and 'oomph' (Arneis from Piedmont is worth a go). But oak is not needed, so Riesling is the best bet. *Chicken and mushroom* likes Chardonnay and Pinot Noir, just as a non-risotto dish might. *Primavera* favours fresh, zingy whites.

Salads A huge subject, that more often than not just needs a spot of common sense. As basic *green* or *mixed* salad is virtually tasteless without dressing, and dressing often contains vinegar, you must dress carefully. People will tell you that light whites are the best. But you are hardly going to order a glass of white to accompany your *pousse and shallot* salad after having downed a rare steak and chips. Just move the salad into view and finish off your red. Don't worry, the salad is a palate cleanser, it knows that it is not the main show. *Seafood* salad enjoys the white wines that go well with seafood (see below); *niçoise* likes tangy Sauvignon Blancs; *chicken* salad works well with Rhône whites and middle-weight Chardonnays; *feta* salad, not surprisingly, is perfect with dry Greek whites; *French bean and shallot* salad likes Alsace Tokay-Pinot Gris and Pinot Blanc; *tomato and basil* salad is best matched with rosé and all things fresh, dry, keenly acidic, Italian and white; *Caesar* salad, if made properly, is great with Sauvignon Blanc; *Waldorf* salad needs softer whites like Alsatian Pinot Blanc and Sylvaner, or South African Chenin Blanc; *pasta* salad can get a little stodgy, so uplifting dry whites again are essential. Every country in the wine world makes salad-friendly wines, even the UK, where the better dry white grapes like Bacchus, Reichensteiner and Seyval Blanc can be a joy. Don't look any further the next time you are out and about.

Sausages (meaty ones as opposed to fish or veggie) Any sausage dish including *toad-in-the-hole* and *bangers and mash* (two of the top ten dishes of all time) need manly, robust, no messin' reds. Cahors, Garnacha from Penedès, Western Australian Shiraz or Cabernet, Malbec from Argentina, any Languedoc or southern Rhône reds, Barbera from northern Italy, Primitivo from southern Italy, Chinon and other red Loires are all suitable. Zinfandel, Merlot and Cabernet from California would be awesome, as would a bottle of claret. Hurrah for sausages and their global compatibility with red wine. My desert island luxury, if ever it came to it, would be soss, mash and Châteauneuf-du-Pape.

Seafood (other than fish and shellfish) Muscadet, Pouilly-Fumé, Sancerre (French), Chenin Blanc (South Africa) Albariño (Spain), Lugana, Verdicchio, Soave and Pinot Grigio (Italy) and any dry

New World, unoaked whites are all compatible with seafood. This is another huge section where thinking the dish through pays dividends. *Squid* and *octopus* both need very dry whites like Sauvignon Blanc, Italian or Spanish whites – and resinous Greek whites if the dish is served in its ink. The curious, bouncy texture of both squid and octopus does not embrace wine in the same way fish does, and so concentrate on the method of cooking and the other ingredients to help you make the final choice. *Crevettes grises* or the little grey/brown shrimps, eaten whole as a pre-dinner nibble, are stunning with Muscadet or Loire Sauvignon Blanc. *Prawns* are a step up in terms of flavour, and dry English whites, simple, dry Riesling, Sémillon/Sauvignon Blanc blends or solo cuvées are all lovely. If you favour a *prawn cocktail* (and I certainly do), then smartish Sauvignon Blanc is dry and aromatic enough to wade through the Marie Rose sauce. *Lobster*, the smartest of all crustaceans, served cold or in a salad, should lead you into the deepest, darkest corners of your cellar to uncork the finest whites. Burgundy (no upper limit), Australian and New Zealand (only the best – not too oaky), Californian Chardonnay (elegant as opposed to blockbuster) and Viognier, from its spiritual birthplace in Condrieu, northern Rhône, will all set you back a fortune. But if you've bought lobster in the first place, then you can go the extra mile and finish the job properly with a great white. *Lobster thermidore* is not my favourite dish, as I feel that lobster loses its magical texture and flavour when it is served hot, but you can easily open up richer (but less expensive) whites like Aussie Sémillons or South American Chardonnays. If you feel like a slice of lobster class, but for a slightly reduced price, then *langoustines* are the answer. Lobster-wines are perfect here, just adjust the prices downwards a few quid. *Dressed crab* is a fabulous dish and once again Loire whites, like Muscadet (only £4 to £5 for a good bottle) is spot on. Dry whites like Ugni Blanc from Gascony, Jurançon and Chablis, are also good, but Sauvignon Blanc is probably the pick of the grapes. Don't just look at the Loire, though, as white Bordeaux and Bergerac often have a fair slug of Sauvignon in them, and Sauvignon is grown all over the New World. *Mussels* probably do best in *gratin* or *marinière* form, when Riesling, Barossa Sémillon, New Zealand Pinot Gris, Sauvignon Blanc (again) and Aligoté are all worthy contenders. *Scallops* can take on a little more weight in a white (mildly oaked Sauvignon Blanc) and even a spot of light red. *Scallops wrapped in bacon* are a wicked combo with smart rosé. *Oysters* are traditionally drunk with Champagne even though I prefer a simple dry white like Muscadet, with its salty tang, or a 'village' Chablis or Petit Chablis. And lastly a *plateau de fruits de mer* – all of the above, plus whelks (yuk) and winkles (what's the point?) and other bits and pieces – really only needs a Sauvignon de Touraine or a bottle of Muscadet. You'll thank me, because after you receive the bill for this bountiful platter of seafood you'll be delighted to spend a fraction of that on a bottle of decent wine. For *clams*, see 'Pasta'.

Side dishes see 'Vegetables'.

Snails see 'Garlic'.

Soups Dry sherry is often quoted as the soup saviour. But I am unlikely to crack open a fresh bottle of fino every time I fancy a bowl of soup, and what's more, it isn't the best wine for the job as the soup family is a diverse collection of individuals and no one wine can do the entire job. *Minestrone* likes to keep things Italian and Teroldego or Marzemino from Trentino would be great. But if you want to hop over the border to France then southern Rhônes would make a nice change. *Spinach and chickpea* soup goes well with bone-dry whites like Orvieto, Frascati, New Zealand, South African or Chilean Sauvignon Blanc. *Vichyssoise* (chilled leek and potato) needs creamy, floral styles of white, like simple Alsatian Riesling, South American or French Viognier or white Rhône. *Lobster* or *crayfish bisque* has a creamy texture and considerable richness so dry sherry could conceivably make an appearance. If you don't fancy that, then white Burgundy is best. *Bouillabaisse (with rouille)*, the serious fish, garlic, tomatoes, onion and herb broth, with floating toasty crostinis topped with garlic, chilli and mayo, is a mighty dish and yet it only needs tiddly little whites like our old favourites Muscadet and Sauvignon de Touraine. *Consommé* is a definite dry sherry dish (at last). *Gazpacho* (chilled tomato, cucumber, onion, pepper and garlic soup) likes nothing more than Spanish mildly oaked Viura. *Mushroom* soup is another dry sherry candidate, while *French onion* soup goes well with dry Riesling from Alsace or South Australia's better regions. *Oxtail* demands hearty reds – rustic, earthy southern French bruisers are inexpensive and ideal for this dish. *Lentil and chestnut* soup and *lentil and bacon* both crave sherry, again, while *clam chowder* is basically a fishy soup with cream (and possibly potato) so Sauvignon Blanc, Chenin Blanc and all seafoody whites are perfect. *Vegetable* soup can be dull, but can also be excellent; either way, rustic reds at the bottom end of the market are sound. *Tomato* soup is a strange one. I favour light reds or dry whites. Avoid oak, Gamay (Beaujolais or Loire) or Sauvignon Blanc (Pays d'Oc, Loire, Chile) all do the job well.

Sweetbreads Classically cooked with butter and sorrel, sweetbreads demand aromatic, richly textured white wines. Alsatian or South Australian Riesling would be my first choices. If you can't find any, then try creamy, oily Rhône whites.

Tapas Sherry and dry white wines, (preferably Spanish and avoid oaky ones) are perfect partners for these tasty Spanish snacks.

Terrines A terrine is really a more robust pâté, generally served in slices. So what is good enough for a pâté is good enough for a terrine. Some of the classics are *ham and chicken*, which loves white Burgundy, or elegant non-French Chardonnays. Another white Burgundy lover is *jambon persillé*, the sublime parsley, jelly and ham dish. Beaujolais, Alsatian Gewürztraminer, Riesling and Tokay-Pinot Gris love *rabbit*, *hare* and *game terrines* particularly if they have prunes lurking within. *Fish terrines* follow the lead of fish pâtés and *mousses* (or is that meece?) with Sauvignon Blanc, Riesling, clean, fresh Chardonnays, like Chablis, and Albariño.

Thai Along the same lines as *Vietnamese* and other 'Asian, but not overly so' styles of cuisine, it is best to look to the main ingredient in each dish and then concentrate on appropriate southern hemisphere fruit-driven wines. Likely candidates are Australian and New Zealand Riesling, Sémillon and Sauvignon Blanc, New World sparkling wines in general, dry Muscat and Pinot Gris from Argentina or the Antipodes.

Tomato Strangely, tomatoes are pretty fussy when it comes to wine-matching (see 'Soup'). Pinot Noir works, but generally New World versions perform better than their Old World counterparts, as they often have more fruit and lower acidity. Other reds like Sicilian Nero d'Avola, Puglian Primitivo (Italy) and any juicy, warm-climate Merlot or Zinfandel are accommodating. When *raw*, as in a salad, rosé is the best choice. A *tomato sauce* demands dry, light whites and Italy is the best place to look for these, as they are often ripe and cheap. *Tomato ketchup*, while delicious, is so sweet and vinegary that it gives wine a hard time, so use sparingly on your burger if you are drinking fine wine. Drench it if you are gunning down a glugger.

Truffles Truffley, foresty, feral and musky. Yum. You have a choice of similarly scented wines to match this; Burgundian Pinot Noir, Piedmont's magnificent Nebbiolo and Syrah (French and posh, please). If you want to cook chicken or fish with truffles then vintage Champagne or top Alsatian Riesling would be spectacular.

Turkey see 'Chicken'.

Turkish I have already covered lamb kebabs (with chilli sauce) in its own special section. But Turkish food is inevitably best with Greek wines (endeavouring to be non-controversial), as the cuisine styles are linked and the resinous whites and purple, scented reds are spot on.

Veal There are some mightily good dishes in this section. And veal really likes to be treated carefully on the wine front, preferring to keep the company of senior white wines and lighter reds. *Saltimbocca*, the epic veal, sage and prosciutto dish, needs a wine to 'jump in the mouth'. Pinot Nero (Italian Pinot Noir) would be just right. If that is hard to find, then Trincadeira from Portugal would be an inexpensive, inspirational substitute. *Vitello tonnato*, the thinly sliced, braised veal, served cold in a marinated sauce of tuna, lemon juice, olive oil and capers, is one of the world's most elegant and tasty starters. Take the tuna and anchovy (used in the braising stage) as your lead. Fresh, sunny, seaside whites like Verdicchio and Vernaccia work especially well. *Wiener schnitzel*, fried veal in egg and breadcrumbs can be on the dry side, so what else is on the plate? Because if there is nothing else of enormous character, then Chardonnay is a winner. *Blanquette de veau*, the French classic with a cream sauce, is definitely a white wine dish. Again Chardonnay (near or far) works, but for perfection, Viognier, Roussanne or Marsanne blends from the Rhône would be exact. *Osso bucco*, a veal shin with wine, tomatoes, parsley, garlic and zesty gremolata, is a lighter, more heady stew than most, and New Zealand, Tasmanian or Oregon Pinot Noir would be great, as would huge, full-on Chardonnays from anywhere.

Vegetables Vegetables (and accompaniments) on the whole are relatively neutral tasting compared to the main dish. But depending on how they are cooked they can require a moment or two's thought. Any *gratin* (baked with cheese), or *dauphinoise* dish needs light reds or self-confident whites on the table. *Beetroot* is a tad tricky, but Alsatian whites generally have the texture and flavour to make it through. *Cabbage, leeks, spinach, parsnips, cauliflower, sprouts, carrots, peas* and *potatoes* are usually innocent, but *gnocchi*, whether plain or flavoured with *spinach*, need juicy, fruit-driven wines to lubricate the palate. *Marinated vegetables* and *polenta* not surprisingly love Italian whites – Pinot Grigio, Soave and so on. *Lentils* dry the palate out and rustic, earthy reds are essential. Look to French Country wines or to Chile and Argentina. *Corn on the cob*, however, is a dead ringer for New World Sauvignon Blanc. Open a bottle and sometimes you'll get a canned sweetcorn aroma!

Vinaigrette A passion killer for a wine as vinegar is so strong that it makes any wine taste flat for a few seconds. Dressing made with lemon juice and oil is more wine-friendly.

Vinegar See above! *Balsamic* vinegar seems to be more wine friendly than most.

Welsh rarebit Always finish on a good note, and cheese on toast is a must for survival. Whether you make these for late night nibbling or as a traditional savoury after pudding, you deserve a meaty little rustic red alongside. Anything from the south of France, Bulgaria, southern Italy or Spain would be a fantastic match.

PUDDINGS

A sweet wine is a super way to finish off a feast and I have outlined a short list of favourite puddings and their dream wines. There is only one rule when matching wine to sweet food. Make sure the wine is at least as sweet as the pudding otherwise the wine will taste dry. Most shops have a few sweet wines, but not as many as one would like. They are often sold in half bottles, which is great as they can easily go around six people and there will be no wastage. You may have to find a decent independent merchant to get a good selection of sweeties (see the 'Directory' pages 161-224). And check out my Top 250 for a comprehensive range of sweet wines that cover all of the dishes in this section.

Almond tart A benchmark dish that, despite its luxurious elements and texture, needs careful handling on the wine front. Lighter sweeties like Muscat de Beaumes-de-Venise, Moelleux (sweet) Loire whites and Jurançons would be a delight. If you have an almondy tart with fresh fruit on top go for similar wines. *Bakewell tart*, while perhaps not as elegant as a fresh fruit tart, will still revel in a gorgeous sweet wine, along the same lines as the above.

Apple *Strudels*, *pies* and *crumbles* enjoy varying degrees of nutty, cinnamony, buttery pastry and brown-sugar-toffee flavours. Without going too crazy, a richer, heavier style of pudding wine is needed. German Riesling, Auslese level and above, late-picked Muscat from Australia, classic French Sauternes or New World botrytised Sémillon and lighter Hungarian Tokaji are all runners. *Baked* apples need ice-cold, light, fresh German or Austrian Riesling, Spätlese or Auslese level. For *tarte tatin* see below.

Apricot A galactically awesome combo is Vendange Tardive (late-picked) Condrieu (from the northern Rhône) and apricot crumble. Unfortunately this sort of wine is rare and exceedingly expensive, so where else should you look? Well, sweet Jurançon is out there, bursting with flavour, and so is Monbazillac, a budget Sauternes-style offering.

Bananas *Raw*, surely it is breakfast, so put the corkscrew down. *Banoffee pie*, the hideous love child of sticky toffee and frisky bananas can only be tamed by the butchest of sweet wines – Hungarian Tokaji, Australian liqueur Muscat and Malmsey Madeira. Good luck. With *banana split*, the toppings and flavours of the ice cream are more dominant than the comedy banana, so tread carefully. Anyway, you shouldn't serve wine at children's birthday parties.

Berries *Black, goose, blue, rasp, logan, huckle* (no joke), *straw, mul, cran, bil* and his mate *damson* pop up in many different guises. But whether they are served *au naturel*, in a *compote*, or in a *summer pudding*, they all love Sémillon and Muscat. Track these grapes down from France – Sauternes, Saussignac, Monbazillac, Loupiac all falling neatly into the Sémillon camp; Muscat de Rivesaltes, de Beaumes-de-Venise, de Frontignon, all advertise the variety Muscat on the label, so are easier to find. Aussie late-picked Muscats are all great, but don't buy liqueur Muscats as they are wildly different.

Biscuits/Biscotti (and proper shortbread) Vin Santo has to be the top choice, with heady sweet wines like Sauternes or New World botrytised Sémillon doing the job admirably. Other, lighter biscuits enjoy the company of simpler sweet wines, but I would stick to Sémillon or Chenin Blanc-based French versions.

Brandy snaps A personal favourite, which is luckily not burdened with brandy. Try Australian liqueur Muscat, you'll love it.

Bread and butter pudding You need wines with a bit of clout for a traditional B&B pudding. Weightier Muscat is my favourite grape for the job – Moscatel de Setúbal from Portugal and Moscato/ Passito di Pantelleria, from an island off Sicily, would both be a delight. A bottle of each guv'nor.

Cakes What is wrong with a cup of tea? Well quite a lot, when you could enjoy a teeny glass of cream sherry or Aussie liqueur Muscat with *coffee cake*, demi-sec Champagne with *Victoria sponge* or Bual Madeira with *Dundee*, *Battenberg*, *brownies* or a traditional *fruit cake*. *Doughnuts* love elephants.

Cherries In *pie* form cherries behave like berries and like mid-weight sweet wines. With *chocolate*, in a *marquise*, or in *Black Forest gâteau* try Amarone, the wickedly rich red wine from Veneto in Italy, or Californian Zinfandel for a bizarre match. It works, honest.

Chocolate *Cake* can, if it is not too intense, retreat into lighter Muscats and botrytised Rieslings. *Chocolate mousse*, *petits pots au chocolat* and *chocolate soufflé* all head towards Orange Muscat, with its pervading aroma and flavour of orange blossom. This is one of the finest food and wine combinations of all, as orange and chocolate are natural partners (just ask Terry). Australia and California make a few and they are superb. Otherwise, Tokaji, black Muscat, liqueur Muscat, PX (short for Pedro Ximénez, the boozy, black, teeth-rottingly sweet turbo-sherry), botrytised Sémillon from the New World, Maury and Banyuls – the mega port-like sweet Grenache wines from the south of France – and finally tawny port are all successful partners.

Christmas pudding It is useful to have a wine that lasts well once opened. And liqueur Muscats from Australia and tawny port, as well as Malmsey Madeira, all fit the bill.

Cheesecake My favourite is cherry, but to be honest it doesn't really matter what fruit you put in them; the cake, not the fruit, controls the choice of wine. Botrytised Sémillon and Riesling from the New World, Coteaux du Layon and other sweet Loire wines, Austrian Beerenauslese Bouvier and Alsatian Vendange Tardive Riesling and Tokay all work. The trick is to keep the sweetness intense, without resorting to a heavyweight style of wine.

Cinnamon rolls A heavenly creation, however eating one should be considered a criminal offence. You need sweetness and toffeed aromas in the wine to cope with the intensity of sugar. Vin Santo, Tokaji, liqueur Muscat and Banyuls would warrant another five years in the slammer. *Lardy cakes* get you in the same trouble, so be prepared.

Crème brûlée As I only like the top crunchy bit as opposed to the silky creamy bit, I can only guess at the best match. I reckon that my almond tart wines, coupled with my cheesecake wines will be somewhere in the zone. And as Loire sweeties, made from Chenin Blanc, appear in both sections, they must be spot on. Coteaux du Layon, Moelleux Vouvrays, Bonnezeaux (pronounced 'Bonzo'!) are your choices.

Crème caramel Another pud that you won't get me near, but I have it on good authority that light, delicate sweeties are the order of the day. German Auslese Rieslings from the Mosel and fresh Muscats would be ideal.

Crêpes Suzette Clairette de Die, the little-known sparkling wine from the Rhône, or Asti from Italy would be the cheaper options, with demi-sec Champagne being the 'with knobs on' choice.

Custard As soon as you wade in with custard on, say, a jam roly-poly, you are giving the wine much more to think about. Creaminess in a dish needs acidity in a wine to counter it, so with custard being the ultimate in eggy creaminess, the big guns like Malmsey Madeira, liqueur Muscat and Tokaji must be released from their cages.

Doughnuts see 'Cakes'.

Fruit Raw fruit of any kind has a much lighter flavour than you would expect when pitted against a sweet wine. Stay very dainty with Asti, German or Austrian Spätlese Rieslings, demi-sec Champagne, fresh Muscats, Italy's Recioto di Soave, Spain's Moscatel de Valencia or light Sauternes. Oh, if you fancy a lychee, then sweet Gewürztraminer is a safe bet, as it has remarkable lychee characteristics on the nose and palate. For *pies* see 'Berries'.

Fruitcake see 'Cakes'.

Gingerbread A wonderful creation that, along with *ginger cake* and *ginger biscuits*, is made even better when accompanied by a glass of Malmsey Madeira.

Gooseberry fool A refreshing pud, which doesn't take to heavy sweet wines. Young, sweet Sémillon, like Sauternes, Saussignac, Monbazillac or Loupiac would be delicious. Just try to keep the price down, as the more expensive wines will usually be more intense. Otherwise grab some fresh young German Riesling for a fruit-cocktail-style flavour.

Ice cream I once did a tasting where rosé Sancerre ended up being the perfect partner for Chunky Monkey. So, as you may be able to guess, matching wine with ice cream it is not always easy. My safest rule is that *vanilla*, *chocolate*, *rum and raisin*, *coffee*, *toffee* and *cookie dough* ice creams love Pedro Ximénez, the intensely coffee and raisiny sweet sherry. You could always try sweet liqueur Muscats from Australia as well. If you have a *fruity ice cream* or *sorbet*, just leave it alone.

Jam tart Very sweet is the only rule, as you can't get sweeter than jam. Icewine (made from pressing grapes that have frozen on the vine) from Canada might be a relatively inexpensive way of tackling this dish.

Jelly German or Austrian light Rieslings should not interfere too much with the jelly. Otherwise you could recreate a kid's tea party and have a fizzy drink (Asti?).

Lemon meringue pie German Riesling or Loire Chenin Blanc handle the citrus theme well. The good thing is that these two styles of wine are relatively inexpensive, and there is, at last, a move back to German wines these days.

Meringue On its own, meringues are virtually tasteless, so when served with fruit (*pavlova*), the fruit is all that concerns you, so see 'Fruit' above.

Mince pies I love to follow the Christmas cake and pudding idea of Madeira, tawny port and liqueur Muscats. It will save you another trip out to the shops. And they are all big enough to wrestle with the brandy butter. They also go a very long way – twelve to fifteen glasses in one bottle.

Pastries Kind of the same school as tarts and cakes, in that you are not really expected to crack open a bottle of wine for a *pain au chocolat*. However, if you are in the mood, then Coteaux du Layon, Muscat de Beaumes-de-Venise, Saussignac and Monbazillac are France's best efforts. Botrytised Riesling from Australia and New Zealand might also work well. Also try German Spätlese Riesling, keeping the price down.

Peach melba Botrytised Riesling does the peachy thing well, so head 'down under' or off to Germany. For *poached peaches* see 'Fruit'.

Pecan pie A well-deserved entry from one of the classic American dishes that strangely needs to be drunk with Australian wine. Magill Tawny, from super-winery Penfold's, is the benchmark wine with this. Otherwise, Aussie liqueur Muscats or, if you fancy something a little posher, Malmsey Madeira, are all delish.

Pineapple upside-down pudding Got to get a mention, as one of the most irresistible menu items of all time. The caramel and pineapple team up to form a fairly exotic partnership in this dish, and smart Sauternes would give a real result here. If you are cutting back, then Australian botrytised Sémillon would also work wonders.

Plum crumble Of the crumble family, plum is up there with blackberry and apple as one of the most fearsome. A bit of concentration is needed (in the wine, not you reader) so head off to Canada for Riesling Icewines or to Italy for heroic Vin Santo.

Rhubarb crumble A relative lightweight next to the plum above, rhubarb crumble likes to take it easy. Exotically sweet Riesling from just about anywhere has a rhubarby nose and palate. So this is the only grape that I would allow.

Rice pudding Cor, I haven't had rice pudding since school, so I don't know. Sorry.

Rum baba By the very nature of the beast, a rum baba has a bit of a kick. Underneath the mild, genial exterior, a sweet-wine-bashing horror is waiting to get out. You have to go for fortified wine to stand a chance, so our front line soldiers, tawny port, Bual or Malmsey Madeira and liqueur Muscat are the best bet we've got.

Sorbet see 'Ice cream'.

Steamed puddings It is quite simple. The greatest form of syrupy, toffee, old-fashioned puddings (spotted dick included) deserves the most regal sweet wines. And they have all been mentioned before – Bual or Malmsey Madeira, Tokaji, Vin Santo and liqueur Muscat.

Strawberries Top quality strawberries absolutely love Asti (Spumante) and Moscato d'Asti, demi-sec Champagne and Clairette de Die. Fizz with a touch of sweetness – perfect for a spot of tennis.

Tarte au citron see 'Lemon meringue pie'.

Tarte tatin Another spectacular dish, but one that doesn't quite fit into the 'Apple' section. (By the way pear tatin is acceptable, pineapple is not!) When cooked to perfection, honeyed Loire sweeties like Coteaux du Layon are right on the button. New World botrytised Sémillons would do, but could be a little clumsy.

Tiramisù A strangely unappetising dish in my opinion, as the coffee and mascarpone and chocolate, with the addition of brandy, never seem to knit together. It is best accompanied by Vin Santo.

Toffee apple see 'Tarte tatin'.

Treacle sponge see 'Steamed puddings'.

Treacle tart Treacle tart, particularly if you have included the lemon zest, is not as stodgy a dish as you might expect. You could try Sauternes, but if in any doubt, then Hungarian Tokaji or liqueur Muscat would probably be safest.

Trifle The marvellous old English creation, adorning sideboards up and down the country, must be delighted to have so many options on the wine front today. German Riesling Beerenauslese would be my pick, but any sweet Riesling would be lovely. Likewise, Sauternes and the family of world-wide sweet Sémillons all love this dish. If tipping in a bit of booze, sherry is traditionally used, and a good quality cream sherry is probably best.

Zabaglione Passito di Pantelleria, from the tiny volcanic island off Sicily, is the only wine to accompany this creamy concoction, unless the Marsala you use in the recipe is drinkable, too.

CHEESE

When considering wine with cheese surprisingly anything goes – white, red, sweet, dry and fortified wines. Keep the cheese board simple to limit the number of flavours and wines and watch out for chutney, as the pungent flavours tend to trip the wine up. I have listed several categories of cheese and some of my favourites in each section.

Fresh cheese (*Cream cheese, feta, ricotta* and *mozzarella*) Usually used in salads or cooking the flavours are not dominant, so drink what you fancy. See 'Cheese (in cooking)'.

Natural rind cheese (*Crottin de Chavignol, Sainte-Maure de Touraine, Saint-Marcellin* and *Selles-sur-Cher*) Light Sauvignon Blanc or Chenin Blanc from the Loire are superb with goat's cheese, with Sancerre being the pick of the crop (Chavignol is one of the finest wine villages in Sancerre and the producer of the famous Crottin). However, any dry, fresh, unoaked white would be fine. If you feel like drinking red, then again Loire Cabernet Franc or Gamay work perfectly.

Soft white cheese (*Camembert, Brie de Meaux, Pavé d'Affinois, Chaource, Bonchester, Pencarreg, Explorateur, Boursault, Gratte-Paille* and *Brillat-Savarin*) Once again, Sauvignon Blanc works terrifically well, although you may want some more 'oomph' so head to New Zealand, South Africa or Australia. The richer the cheese, the bigger the white, so Chardonnay can be considered, too. Reds that work are Pinot Noir (either red Sancerre or lighter red Burgundies), fresh young Rhône Syrah and rosé Champagne, while the Gratte-Paille and Brillat-Savarin go well with youthful, inexpensive claret.

Washed rind cheese The milder examples like *Chaumes, Port Salut* and *Milleens* like nothing more than dry, fruity reds – light Loire red or Bordeaux, for example. The smellier cheeses, including *Epoisses, Chambertin* and *Langres*, really enjoy white Burgundy, Alsace Riesling or Tokay and other controlled (not too oaky) Chardonnays from further afield. *Munster* loves Alsatian Gewürztraminer and *Vacherin Mont d'Or* loves red Burgundy, Beaujolais and lighter red Rhônes.

Semi-soft cheese A huge selection of cheese. Try the following combinations: *Livarot* – Alsatian Tokay Pinot-Gris; *Maroilles* – Roussanne or Marsanne from the Rhône; *Pont-l'Evêque* – Viognier, also from the Rhône; *Raclette* – assuming you are reading this on skiing holiday, anything from the Savoie, red or white; *Gubbeen* – Pinot Blanc or Sylvaner from Alsace; *Edam* – whatever, it likes light whites and reds; *Morbier* – Rhône whites; *Fontina* – light, Alpine Gamay; *Reblochon* – much richer Gamay from Beaujolais and red Burgundy; *Saint-Nectaire* – the same again, plus Côtes-du-Rhône; *Tomme de Savoie* – either Rhône whites or lighter reds; *Bel Paese* and *Taleggio* – Lombardy whites like Lugana, and reds like Franciacorta; *Milleens* – needs gutsier whites or light fresh reds.

Hard cheese The largest category of all, that ranges from mild, via medium to strong and extra-strong cheeses. Suffice to say get an idea of the strength of your chosen cheese and this will help your wine selection. Cheeses in this group are, among others – *Cheddar, Gruyère, Cheshire, Parmigiano-Reggiano, Pecorino, Cornish Yarg, Double Gloucester, Lancashire, Caerphilly, Gouda, Beaufort, Lancashire, Manchego, Cantal, Etorki, Comté, Emmental, Jarlsberg, Mimolette*. From mild to extra strong, the wines to go for are: **Whites** – Alsace Pinot Blanc, Chablis, Jurançon Sec, white Burgundy, white Rhônes, New World Chardonnays; **Reds** – Loire reds, Chilean Merlot, Côtes-du-Rhône, spicy Italian reds like Primitivo, Old World Cabernet from Bordeaux or New World from Margaret River (Australia), Shiraz from Clare Valley (Australia), Vino Nobile di Montepulciano and Chianti (Italy) and Zinfandel (California); **Fortified** – Port (tawny, LBV and vintage), Madeira, Banyuls and Maury (both from France) and old oloroso sherries.

Blue cheese *Stilton* loves Madeira, tawny Port and LBV or vintage Port; *Roquefort* and *Fourme d'Ambert* are dead keen on Sauternes, Monbazillac or Saussignac; *Dolcelatte* is a bit of a lightweight and because of its unusual sweet flavour and texture, I'd leave it alone; *Gorgonzola* likes Amarone della Valpolicella; *Chashel Blue* likes sweet whites and *Beenleigh Blue* must, just must, have cider (I thought I should not end on a wine!).

THE TOP 250

£6.99 **Hardy's Nottage Hill Brut Chardonnay**, NV, Southeast Australia, Australia (**Bot, Saf, Sai, Thr, WCe and WRa**). Creamy, pineappley, soft and luscious, this wine has lovely texture and a smooth, fruity finish. If you are not a fan of perkily acidic sparkling wine, then Nottage Hill is the right choice for you as it is mild and melodious. However, it is not a wine for cocktails as you need more racy acidity for Kir Royales etc. The main reason to go for this is that it is a crowd-pleaser; it is inexpensive and it is so easy to drink!

£7.99 **Prosecco Santo Stefano, Ruggeri, Valdobbiadene**, NV, Veneto, Italy (**Valvona & Crolla and Wimbledon**). This single vineyard Prosecco is fizzy, refreshing and dry, tempered by a tiny touch of residual sugar that comes through on the finish as a juicy grapey highlight. Prosecco is the wine that is traditionally combined with white peach pulp to make a Bellini cocktail. But I wouldn't use this version, as it is far too delicious. Not as aggressively fizzy as Champagne this prickly wine is a nice drink to unwind to after a hard day's work.

£8.90 **Davenport Brut**, NV, Kent, England (**Davenport Vineyards**). I tasted a sample bottle of this vintage fizz just minutes after it left the bottling line. Not exactly ideal conditions for an assessment, but, considering it hadn't even had a chance to gather itself, let alone grab some clothing (a label and capsule), it tasted superb. Will Davenport's inexpensive sparkling wine is a landmark. It is refreshing, dry and creamy, and the bubbles last for ages.

One of my acid tests for a fizz is to look for thin, continuous streams of tiny bubbles rising up through the glass – a mark of excellence. And there they were. The group of microscopic snorkelers, perusing the bottom of my glass. Order from info@davenportvineyards.co.uk

£9.99 **Chandon Australia**, NV, Victoria, Australia (**Saf, Unw and Wai**). This is a wonderfully creamy, rich style of fizz from the Yarra Valley-based branch of Moët & Chandon. With Dom Pérignon in their portfolio (albeit a long way away in Champagne), you should expect this wine to live up to pretty high standards, and it does. It is made in the traditional (Champagne) method from Chardonnay and Pinot Noir. The grapes are sourced from far and wide, including the unlikely sounding viticultural area of Strathbogie. The result is the best value sparkling wine ever to have come out of Australia.

£9.99 **Jansz**, NV, Tasmania, Australia (**Carringtons, Corks, Charles Hennings, Odd, Peckham & Rye, Thos Peatling, Selfridges, Vin du Van and Noel Young**). Jansz NV in my opinion is the better of the two Jansz wines. The vintage is three or four pounds more, and usually vintage sparklers have the edge on the non-vintages. But in this case, the classically produced, NV blend of 58% Chardonnay, 40% Pinot Noir, 2% Pinot Meunier is the winner. The finesse and elegance of this wine belies its sub-tenner price. The creamy, citrus fruit is refreshing, balanced and uplifting; in fact it is a joy.

£11.99 **Green Point by Chandon**, 1997, Victoria, Australia (**Adnams, Bot, Odd, Tes, Unw, Wai and WRa**). This is the big brother of the Chandon Australia wine, with more weight, structure and length of flavour. If Chandon is a party-type fizz then Green Point is a dinner party style. You could be fooled into thinking this wine is a lot more expensive than it tastes. As there is so much dodgy Champagne out there, you would be wise to avoid any unknown labels and spend your money on this.

£11.99 **Pelorus, Cloudy Bay**, NV, Marlborough, New Zealand (**Adnams, Corks, General Wine, Harvey Nichols, S.H. Jones, Lay & Wheeler, Peckham & Rye, Philglas, Selfridges and Wimbledon**). The new cuvée of this wine features about 20 % Pinot Noir. It used to be a Blanc de Blancs (100% Chardonnay), but in order to fatten up the middle palate, the Pinot has been brought in. And a good job it does, too. The mega-famous Cloudy Bay guys make this ultra-chic wine and it rocks. You will be seeing it at parties all over the country soon.

£14.95 **Claude Carré, Blanc de Blancs**, NV, Champagne, France (**General Wine**). I have been following (and drinking) this Champagne for nearly a decade. It is made from 100% Chardonnay and comes from the small village of Trépail. Trépail is firmly in the red grape (Pinot Noir) zone of Champagne, but Claude's vines are right on the top of a hill, above the frost line, and they are all, unusually, Chardonnay. His vineyard situation is most easily explained

as a nipple of Chardonnay on a breast of Pinot Noir. Carré's
wine has always been a stunner, but recently, thanks to a
strong pound, it is a complete bargain, offering creamy,
persistent, nutty, yeasty fruit, with a heroic dry finish.

£14.99 **Pierre Gimonnet, Cuis 1er Cru, Blanc de
Blancs**, NV, Champagne, France (**Odd**). This 100%
Chardonnay wine comes from a premier cru-rated village
on the Côte des Blancs. The Gimonnets are perfectionists
and this wine shows how serious they are about their craft.
It is rich but exhibits finesse, it has structure but remains
elegant, in fact they do a superb job of balancing all of the
elements within this delicious Champagne. The great news
is that, as they are not a famous name and don't blow loads
of francs on advertising, their wine is terrific value. Hurrah.

£16.85 **Gatinois Grand Cru, Aÿ**, NV, Champagne, France
(**Haynes, Hanson & Clark**). Some of Pierre Cheval's top
Pinot Noir grapes find their way into Bollinger's best wines.
He is based in Aÿ, the same village as Bolly, and sells them a
proportion of his harvest each year. He keeps the remainder
for his own label, Gatinois. So it follows that Gatinois is
worth a sniff. And, by golly, it is a wonderful wine. A frenzy
of awesome, concentrated Pinot power, with unfettered
extract and weight. If you have ever enjoyed Bollinger, or
any of the other robust, red-grape-heavy styles, then you
will love this wine. The fact that it costs less than a bottle
of one of the shockingly underperforming brands makes
this even easier to swallow.

£17.99 **Pirie**, 1996, Tasmania, Australia (**Boo, D. Byrne and Mill Hill**). For me, this is one of the best sparkling wines made outside of Champagne. Winemaker Dr Andrew Pirie has taken his time in perfecting this classic blend of 70% Pinot Noir and 30% Chardonnay. First made as an experiment in 1993, there is now no doubt as to Tasmania's sparkling wine potential. The totally serious, complex flavours will fox even the most confirmed Champagne *aficionado*. Pirie has haunting nuances of butterscotch, early morning bakery, vanilla, wild honey and lemon curd. It is very yummy indeed.

£21.99 **Billecart-Salmon, Brut Réserve**, NV, Champagne, France (**Adnams, Bentalls, Berry Bros., deFINE, Ben Ellis, Fortnum & Mason, Harvey Nichols, Justerini & Brooks, Lea & Sandeman, James Nicholson, Odd, Peckham & Rye, Roberson, Selfridges, Uncorked and Valvona & Crolla**). I am a fairly harsh critic when it comes to tasting Champagne. For a style of wine that invariably costs a bomb, I am often left underwhelmed by bottles of overly acidic, unripe fizz. Non-vintage Champagne should taste the same whether drinking it in Epernay or Epping. So I drink Billecart. It tastes delicious, year in, year out, on Thursday, at Christmas or Valentine's, in Sydney or Sydenham. It is always fresh, floral, ripe and creamy, and you can't ask for any more than consistent excellence.

£23.99 **R de Ruinart Brut**, NV, Champagne, France (**Bot, Fortnum & Mason, Jeroboams, Lay & Wheeler, Peckham & Rye, Arthur Rackham, Soho Wine, Vintage House,**

Willoughbys, WRa and WCe). My philosophy behind non-vintage Champagne is that it should be refreshing, lively, celebratory and uplifting and this wine is just that. It will make you happy and at the same time reward your taste buds with beautifully balanced flavours that will caress the palate and soothe the spirit. Remember, you don't need a special occasion to open a bottle of Champagne.

£25.99 **Bollinger, Special Cuvée**, NV, Champagne, France (**Asd, Berry Bros., Boo, Bot, Corney & Barrow, Rodney Densem, Direct Wine Shipments, Justerini & Brooks, Lea & Sandeman, Maj, Mor, Odd, Playford Ros, Saf, Sai, Selfridges, Tanners, Tes, Thr, Unw, Valvona & Crolla, Wai, WCe and WRa**). You can buy this wine almost everywhere, so there is no excuse. For all-out, no holds barred, non-vintage Champagne you have to choose Bolly. The richness and yeastiness comes from a time spent in oak barrels, the power from their superb source of first-class grapes and their fabulous reserve wines. Bolly is unique, faultless and memorable. This is a wine drinker's Champagne house and be prepared for a surprise if it is your first go at Bollinger – the wine is magnificently decadent.

£29.95 **Gosset Grande Réserve Brut,** NV, Champagne, France (**Clifton, Corney & Barrow, Fortnum & Mason, Handford, Haslemere Cellar, Pierre Henck, Charles Hennings, Lay & Wheeler, Lea & Sandeman, Mill Hill, Roberson, Scatchard, Sommelier and Whitebridge**). Ignore the perfectly sound Gosset Brut Excellence and trade up five quid or so to the Grande Réserve. In the same way that Billecart N-F (see page 71) is my Cristal or DP, Grande Réserve is my Krug. You are paying under half the price and getting an immensely complex, serious wine with smooth, yeasty, creamy richness and a wickedly long aftertaste. I know it seems blasé to blast the *prestige cuvées*. And if I had the money I am sure I would be uncorking them, too. But in my job I search out the very best regardless of price, reputation and advertising budget. And this wine is near the top of the pile.

£29.99 **Laurent-Perrier, Ultra Brut**, NV, Champagne, France (**Adnams, Corney & Barrow, Fortnum & Mason, Terry Platt, Selfridges, House of Townend, Odd and Uncorked**). I remember a time when this noble Champagne was cult drinking. Aficionados favoured it over its dreary relation, the 'Brut'. For some reason Laurent-Perrier have decided that it needs another push, as it seems to have lost a bit of ground. So what is Ultra Brut? It is a 'non-dosage' style of Champagne – no sugar is added to lift the palate. The result is masterful; intensely flavoured, nutty and yeasty with a long, Saharan-dry finish. I opened this wine with a keen, amateur wine enthusiast pal of mine and he declared it one of the best Champagnes he had ever tasted.

£32.99 **Billecart-Salmon, Brut Rosé** NV, Champagne, France (**Bentalls, Berry Bros., deFINE, Ben Ellis, Fortnum & Mason, Harvey Nichols, Justerini & Brooks, Lea & Sandeman, James Nicholson, Odd, Roberson, Selfridges,**

Uncorked and Valvona & Crolla). This is my favourite rosé Champagne. It is not as rich as Laurent-Perrier (or as expensive) but it is, for me, the epitome of elegance, poise and refinement. Rosé Champagne should not be reserved exclusively for Valentine's Day. It is an all-year-round style that complements food, adds a touch of style to an occasion and ultimately sends signals that you are somebody who has taste and confidence in their own palate. Oh, and the ladies love it (did I blow it all at the end?).

£37.99 **Billecart-Salmon, Cuvée Nicolas-François Billecart**, 1995, Champagne, France (**Berry Bros., deFINE, Ben Ellis, Fortnum & Mason, James Nicholson, Odd, Selfridges and Uncorked**). Billecart can do no wrong, and with their vintage wine, sold for thirty-five pounds cheaper than Dom Pérignon, and forty pounds cheaper than Cristal, it looks and tastes like a steal. Hey, I have just saved you a fortune. Go and spend the money on another bottle – two for one – no contest. 1995 N-F is a truly distinguished wine. I have tasted every vintage of it ever made and the '95 is up there with the best. Serious complexity, richness and a heroic length make this wine the discerning wine lover's secret weapon.

£45.99 **Bollinger, Grande Année**, 1995, Champagne, France (**Asd, Berry Bros., Boo, Bot, Corney & Barrow, Rodney Densem, Direct Wine Shipments, Justerini & Brooks, Lea & Sandeman, Maj, Odd, Playford Ros, Sai, Selfridges, Tanners, Tes, Thr, Unw, WCe and WRa**). The magnificent 1992 Bolly was a hard act to follow (some of the merchants mentioned have a few bottles left). It was a difficult vintage and Bolly came out on top. But 1995 is a stormer of a year and Grande Année is a work of art, with a rich, yeasty, biscuity nose opening out to an elegant, yet mouth-filling, floral palate. There is both power and subtlety in this stunningly balanced wine, and there are very few wines on the shelves with the weight that Bolly engenders. Just wait for the adrenaline rush you'll get when the cork eases out of the bottle.

£2.99 **Safeway Irsai Olivér**, 2000, Neszmély, Hungary (**Saf**). My tasting note for this wine reads: herbal, tropical, v. cheap, Muscat-style?, interesting, creamy, fairly rich and v. cheap. Repetitive, but I couldn't avoid the most obvious attributes of this Hungarian wine. It is very cheap and delightfully fruit-driven. It is not dissimilar to Muscat in grapey flavour and texture, and it edges towards some of the more exotic tastes associated with New World wines, yet manages to remain dry and mouth-filling. It is, perhaps, a little too assertive for an apéritif; however, uncork it with Asian food and it would be a dream. I am delighted with my very first Irsai Olivér, and I hope you are, too.

£3.99 **Domaine Galetis Chardonnay/Viognier**, 2000, Vin de Pays d'Oc, France (**M&S**). Galetis is a stunner of a wine and is definitely one of the best value whites I have ever tasted. The Viognier element is evident on the peachy, tropical fruit nose. Thereafter the Chardonnay takes over, giving the flavour a full, soft, round, pear and honey feel. This grape teamwork produces a fabulous combination of aroma and texture – even the bottle itself oozes style. Galetis is enormously competent when matching to food. This wine is unmissable, so if you are near a branch of M&S, don't delay. Get your hands on this celestial being for less than the price of a TV dinner.

£3.99 **Segada Vinho Branco, Fernão Pires**, 2000, Ribatejo, Portugal (**D. Byrne and Odd**). You will find the red version of this wine later on in the book, so this formidable duo has got to be one of the best value teams on the shelves today. Racy and vibrant, this inexpensive Portuguese white is equally at home as an apéritif or a starters-style wine. The thirst-quenchingly citrus-and-apple palate sets your mouth buzzing and I guarantee that you will get to the bottom of the bottle in record time.

£3.99 **Touraine Sauvignon, Le Chaloutier**, 2000, Loire, France (**Sai**). All things green, wrapped up in a bottle, and a very smart one at that, is my summary of this wine. Asparagus, freshly mown grass, limes, elderberry cordial, gooseberry fool, and a mezzaluna blade coated with chopped herbs, are all available for sniffing on the wine's explosive nose. The astonishing thing is that they are all assembled for a teeny, sub-four-pound price tag.

£3.99 **Zagara Catarratto/Chardonnay, Firriato**, 2000, Sicily, Italy (**Wai**). Zagara uses the little-known native Sicilian grape Catarratto and blends it with world-famous Chardonnay to create a really juicy little wine. This is a super value, fresh, clean, easy-drinking style that could be used as an apéritif or starters-style white. The apple-and-pear-flavoured mid-palate and honeyed finish are spot on, so if you fancy a go at Catarratto, try this.

£4.49 **Bodegas Navasqüés Blanco**, 2000, Navarra, Spain (**UK agents – Stokes 020 8944 5979**). Give Stokes a ring to find out where this wine will be sold. It is a fun white, with clean, herbal, exotic fruit, a touch of honey and a buzzy, dry

LIGHT, DRY AND UNOAKED

finish. Made from Viura, without the intervention of oak, the fruit and finish are really attractive, and for once we do not have to go for a Chardonnay or Sauvignon to taste a serious dry, modern, crowd-pleasing wine.

£4.79 **Domaine Spiropoulos, Mantinia**, 2000, Peloponnese, Greece (**Odd**). Organically produced and bursting with clean, crisp, herbal fruit, this inexpensive Greek offering is remarkably addictive. The fresh acidity makes it a thirst-quenching wine and the finish is long. But it is the unusually tangy, herbal palate that keeps you popping back for a sip. So in no time at all, you've polished off a schooner-sized glass and probably debated the merits of unpronounceable Greek grapes and regions.

£4.99 **Argento Chardonnay**, 2001, Mendoza, Argentina (**Asd, Bibendum, Sai and Tes**). This is the third vintage of Argento and it just gets better and better. Related to the stupendous Alamos (see white – oaked), but much more tangy and edgy, the theme here is pristine, golden lime juice and immense charm. The wine sees a bit of oak, but you wouldn't know it (so I have put it in this section) as the spearmint freshness is invigorating and refreshing. The bottle looks smart and the price is keen, so you can't go wrong.

£4.99 **Jindalee Chardonnay**, 2000, Murray Darling, New South Wales, Australia (**Mor, Saf, Som and Unw**). A friendly new wine that is creamy and full, but not oaky or overblown. It is a versatile style that is light enough to be drunk without food, but cook up a dish and it will muck in and support the flavours. Designed to appeal to as many palates as possible, this wine has certainly achieved its aim. There is also a cheeky Merlot in the Jindalee family, which endeavours to perform the same task for red wine drinkers. I am pleased to report that it also comes up trumps.

£4.99 **Norton Torrontes**, 2001, Mendoza, Argentina (**Odd and WCe**). Weird and wonderful are the two key words to describe this wine. Torrontes is the name of a white grape variety with supposedly Spanish origins that performs tremendously well in Argentina. There are a few versions around on the shelves, but most lack true character and are a bit dull. This wine, however, is zesty, pine-fresh, tropical and citrusy with a superb perky nose and taut, cleansing finish. Read on for another unusual Norton wine in the Red Medium Weight section.

£5.49 **Peter Lehmann Sémillon**, 1999, Barossa Valley, South Australia, Australia (**Asd, Odd, Saf, Sai and Unw**). Peter Lehmann virtually put Sémillon, as a named varietal, on the map. At a remarkable fiver price point, he, year after year, conjures up the most heavenly, lime juice-scented, dry, mouth-filling brew around. The trick with this grape is to pack the glass with ripe tropical flavours and at the same time retain the fresh, citrusy backbone of the variety. This has, as usual, been achieved with style here. Metronomic precision.

£5.50 **Davenport Horsmonden Dry**, 1999, Kent,
England (**Davenport Vineyards**). I tried so hard to find a
Jurançon Sec for this list, as I mention this style of wine
in my 'Food and Wine' section several times. Sadly, only
a few Jurançons make their way over to the UK. They are
dear and on the whole rewarding, but if I could tempt you
to try this wine, Jurançon Sec could become a thing of the
past. Just imagine having an inexpensive English white
that did that same stone fruit, bone-dry, floral, taut,
ethereal thing. This wine does, and it is breathtakingly
beautiful to boot. Who says the manufacturing industry
in the UK is dead? Well, against the might of the
international wine scene, UK winemakers are going for
it and achieving some notable successes. Order from
info@davenportvineyards.co.uk (although Waitrose are
sniffing around, and, as they are arbiters of good taste, you
might find it there soon).

£5.96 **Xanadu, Secession Sémillon/Chardonnay**,
2000, Western Australia, Australia (**Asd and Som**). This
is the white sister to the red Secession, featured later on
in this section. It is a smashing little wine, with a cool
bottle design and racy flavour. Sémillon/Chardonnay
blends used to be everywhere several years ago but they
seem to have disappeared now, which is a shame as these
two grapes are the Thelma and Louise of the wine world.
Zesty, with a citrus theme and perky acidity, Xanadu will
titillate your palate rather than blowing you away. A bit
like the aforementioned heroines.

LIGHT, DRY AND UNOAKED

teeth-tinglingly dry

£5.99 **Antipodean Unwooded Chardonnay**, 1999,
Eden Valley, South Australia, Australia (**Odd**). This Aussie
wine, made by Yalumba, is an unoaked, or 'unwooded'
Chardonnay. Chablis lovers take note. Yalumba have made
a dead ringer to the great French favourite, albeit with the
jazziest capsule on the shelves. Lovely, light floral notes on
the nose are followed by a honeyed mid-palate with
restrained tropical nuances and the essential dry, thirst-
quenching finish. A few pounds cheaper and a few degrees
riper than the real thing, this is a winner.

£5.99 **Frascati Superiore, Selezione Verde,
Pallavicini**, 2000, Lazio, Italy (**Unw**). Frascati is often
desperately dilute, fiercely acidic and lacking in any real
class or charm. But, hurrah, this is a stylish Frascati indeed.
Pallavicini's excellent, retro offering is balanced and fruity,
complex and, in short, a stunner. Malvasia is the grape
variety used and, in this Frascati at least, you can taste
subtle nuances of pear, apple, peach, walnut, honey and
nutmeg. You know that Frascati deserves another chance,
so put the famous name back on track with this wine.

£5.99 **Veramonte Sauvignon Blanc**, 2001, Casablanca,
Chile (**UK agents – Stokes 020 8944 5979**). Veramonte
Sauvignon is teeth-tinglingly dry with a citrus theme. It
would be perfect as an apéritif, or delicious with seafood
dishes. The tangy fruit will effortlessly cut through any
plateau de fruits de mer and seamlessly waltz around a
selection of canapés.

LIGHT, DRY AND UNOAKED

£6.99 **Dashwood Sauvignon Blanc**, 2001, Marlborough, New Zealand (**Bot, Odd, Thr and WRa**). I am a huge fan of the 2001 vintage of Kiwi Sauvignon. Here, the top team at Vavasour Winery's sister label, Dashwood, has made a complete stonker of a wine. The lime juice and mango fruit leaps out of the glass, dives up your nostrils and pulverises your olfactory system into submission. A nerve-janglingly tangy finish follows a fruit bowl of a mid-palate. This is the ultimate apéritif crowd-pleaser.

£6.99 **Mission Hill Private Reserve Pinot Blanc**, 2000, Okanagan Valley, British Columbia, Canada (**Wai**). I first tasted Mission Hill wines while on holiday in Canada and prayed that somebody would import them into the UK. Yippee, they are here and I am doing my level best to keep their sales figures healthy by consuming a ton of bottles myself. Mission Hill's Pinot Blanc is actually one of the best versions of this grape I have ever come across. Even the expensive, exclusive Alsatian producers struggle to compete. Fresh and clean, with a beautiful, creamy texture and no pervasive oak barrel flavours to be seen, this is a celestial creation that will appeal to anybody who likes dry white wine – that's all of you.

£6.99 **Soave Classico Monte Fiorentine, Ca' Rugate**, 2000, Veneto, Italy (**Unw and Valvona & Crolla**). This is serious Soave. 'What?' I hear you cry, 'since when has the summer-glugger Soave been considered a serious wine?' I have been a huge fan of Ca' Rugate since the wine wizards at Valvona & Crolla in Edinburgh introduced me to this estate's grand wines several years ago. But sadly, I had not tasted their wines since, until the ever-vigilant team at Unwins snapped up a parcel of the wonderful Monte Fiorentine. This single vineyard Soave is rich, concentrated, mouth-filling, full and decadent and, what's more, there is not a trace of oak. The price is a bargain for such complexity and intensity of flavour and if you are searching for life beyond Chardonnay and Sauvignon Blanc, this Garganega will surely end your quest.

£7.15 **Quincy, Cuvée Villalin, Domaine Jacques Rouzé**, 2000, Loire, France (**Haynes, Hanson & Clark**). Absolute crispness, pinpoint freshness, nervy acidity and raucous vivacity sum up this tremendous Quincy (pronounced 'can-see'). Rouzé is the main man in this small village, neighbouring Sancerre. Made from top-drawer Sauvignon Blanc vines, Cuvée Villalin will rip your taste buds apart and then reassemble them for you.

£7.49 **Mâcon-Davayé, Domaine des Deux Roches**, 2000, Burgundy, France (**Berry Bros. and Odd**). Made by one of the most reliable estates in the Mâconnais, this delightful, sun-kissed Chardonnay is elegant, balanced and immensely satisfying. The easy-going nature seems to mirror that of the winemaker Jean-Luc Terrier. White Burgundy can often be said to be overpriced and disappointing. This Mâcon is honeyed, floral and crisp, and not too punishing on the wallet. What more could you ask for?

LIGHT, DRY AND UNOAKED

£7.99 Neil Ellis Groenekloof Sauvignon Blanc,
2000, West Coast, South Africa (**Stevens Garnier,
Christopher Piper, Sommelier Wine and Villeneuve**). Neil
Ellis continues to produce some of the most beautiful wines
in the Cape. He weaves into this all of the citrus,
elderflower and asparagus flavours that you would expect.
He also manages to capture a lively spritziness on the
palate, making this an uplifting and refreshing fruit cocktail
of a wine. It is a shame that we can't get a wider range of
Neil's wines in this country, as they are all spectacular. Keep
your eyes peeled though, because things may change in the
future!

**£7.99 Verdicchio dei Castelli di Jesi Classico,
Umani Ronchi**, 2000, Marche, Italy (**Valvona & Crolla
and Wimbledon**). A lovely vibrant, single vineyard
Verdicchio with clean, fresh floral, unoaked fruit and a
lemony, zesty finish. This white is tailor-made for fish dishes
and will provide you with more charm and texture than
most bottles of Chablis. Remember the Umani Ronchi team,
as they are top performers, and there has never been a
better bottle of Verdicchio.

£7.99 Wither Hills Sauvignon Blanc, 2001, Marlborough,
New Zealand (**Great Western, Odd, Edward Sheldon,
T & W, Wai and Wine Society**). This wine is set to scoop
every Sauvignon award available. I tasted the very first
'01 sample available in the UK with Brent Marris, the
winemaker, and even he was gob-smacked by how amazing

it is. The nose leaps gazelle-like from the glass. It is wonderfully pungent, bursting with herbal notes, green pepper, lime zest and papaya overlaying a steely, energetic palate. But if you think the nose is astounding, the finish is nothing short of epic. The addition of 5% barrel-fermented fruit has not only broadened the palate but also stretched the aftertaste out to world record proportions. Monumental.

£8.13 **Roero Arneis, Bric Cenciurio**, 2000, Piedmont, Italy (**Bibendum**). It is rare to find a spectacular Arneis, as few people make this beguiling grape and few estates ship their wine into the UK. This new arrival has serious balance and fabulous depth and intensity, with pure, rich greengage and quince fruit, and no trace of oak. Fans of all things Italian must make it their quest to uncork a bottle.

£8.25 **Chablis, Domaine Daniel Dampt**, 2000, Burgundy, France (**Haynes, Hanson & Clark**). Clean, fresh, no oak, unadulterated, virginal Chardonnay, untouched by new-fangled techniques, delivered to you in a handy glass vessel, known as a bottle, in perfect nick. Taste the purity of this grape variety. It just does not taste like this anywhere else in the world. As a customer at a wine bar once said, 'I hate Chardonnay, but I love Chablis'. Funny hey, as all Chablis is 100% Chardonnay. But in truth I think they meant that sweaty oaky, flabby Chardonnay is grim, but Chablis somehow isn't. Or maybe I'm just wrong. Whatever, this Chablis from Dampt is pinpoint accurate; I want to fill a swimming pool with it, and dive in.

LIGHT, DRY AND UNOAKED

£8.49 **Pouilly-Fumé, Les Cornets, Patrick Coulbois**, 2000, Loire, France (**Asd**). This is an exceptionally versatile Sauvignon Blanc. You can uncork it as a posh apéritif or try it with almost any starter. Crack it open with any fish main course or if you fancy cheese, get hold of some goat – you will be delighted. The amazing thing is that while Les Cornets commands an eight-pound price tag, it sits squarely up there with almost any of its neighbouring estates, and they rarely get an outing below a tenner.

£8.75 **Sancerre, Domaine Etienne Daulny**, 2000, Loire, France (**Haynes, Hanson & Clark**). Three cheers for old-fashioned Sancerre. The kind of wine that makes you sit up straight and grin ear to ear. The crisp, keen, nervy acidity of the Sauvignon Blanc grape courses around your palate, waking up each and every taste bud and giving them all a good kicking. Sancerre, over the last decade, has become the archetypal lunchtime wine, whose soft, pulpy, vaguely refreshing flavours have washed down many a rocket and Parmesan salad. But the time has come to welcome back the old breed of Sancerre, whose fine, leggy, edgy qualities will put Sauvignon Blanc back on everybody's wish list.

£8.99 **Jackson Estate Sauvignon Blanc**, 2000, Marlborough, New Zealand (**Boo, Dorchester, Maj, Odd, Oxford Wine, Philglas, Christopher Piper, Portland, Tanners, Tes, T & W, Wai and Wright**). Most New Zealand Sauvignons change vintage around November. The 2001 wines flood in and we are all immediately entranced by the zingiest, most tropical wines on the planet. However, Jackson Estate hangs around until well into the New Year before switching over. They like to keep their wine in NZ for an extra few months to allow it to knit together and settle down. It is one of the few Kiwi Sauvignons that ages well. So I am delighted to recommend the 2000 Jackson, a complex, classy, broader style that has not been guzzled too young and is now reaching its peak.

£8.99 **Nepenthe Pinot Gris, Adelaide Hills**, 2001, South Australia, Australia (**Odd and Terry Platt**). Serious fruit and superb balance are consummately captured by this epic Pinot Gris. The variety is creeping into vineyards all over the world, but some of the elite offerings (outside of its home in Alsace) are emerging from the Adelaide Hills. So for more structure than Sauvignon, less oak than Chardonnay, less overt fruit than Riesling and more elegance than Sémillon, in short the sort of flavour that really hits the spot with keen wine drinkers, this grape has it all. Take the plunge with Nepenthe's awesome example.

£8.99 **Nepenthe Sauvignon Blanc, Adelaide Hills**, 2000, South Australia, Australia (**Bacchanalia, Evertons, Goedhuis, Great Western, Odd, Terry Platt, Playford Ros, Roberts & Speight, Saf and Wai**). Peter Leske is a genius. He's the bloke behind the taste of Nepenthe and rather than give him seven places in my Top 250 (which they deserve), I am limiting them to three. But in case you are interested, Nepenthe Pinot Noir, Sémillon, unwooded Chardonnay and Fugue (Cab/Merlot) are all brilliant as well. So back to the Sauvignon, which sits squarely between the Loire and Marlborough. (Not geographically – tastewise!) Ripe and vaguely tropical, the acidity in this wine is mouthwatering and drags you through a floral palate of citrus fruit seasoned with a touch of freshly mown grass. Try it if you dare. Mmmmm.

£8.99 **Somerset Hill Unwooded Chardonnay**, 2000, Denmark, Western Australia, Australia (**Odd**). For a Chardonnay that hasn't seen an oak barrel, this is indeed a rich and creamy offering. The fabulous intensity of fruit is tropical and honeyed, with a crisp, refreshing, zippy finish. I realise that not everybody likes overt oak on white wines, so this is probably as good as New World, unoaked Chardonnay gets. It is like super-charged Chablis!

£8.99 **Starvedog Lane Sauvignon Blanc**, 2001, Adelaide Hills, South Australia, Australia (**Amps, D. Byrne, Inspired, Jeroboams, Noble Rot, Saf, Sommelier and Noel Young**). This youthful Sauvignon comes from the super-trendy, boutique winery region of Adelaide Hills. It is a crystal clear, zesty, zingy, citrusy, pineappley glugger. Designed for its immediate thirst-quenching properties and packaged beautifully with a zany label, it is set to be the coolest apéritif of 2002. You will no doubt see the bottle in the hottest bars all over the country.

LIGHT, DRY AND UNOAKED

£9.95 **Isabel Sauvignon Blanc**, 2001, Marlborough,
New Zealand (**Bacchanalia, Bennetts, Butlers, Cheshire
Smokehouse, Cochonnet, deFINE, Fortnum & Mason,
Handford, Charles Hennings, Hoults, Just in Case, Martinez,
Noble Rot, Oxford Wine Co., Philglas, Portland Wine, R.S.
Wines, La Réserve, Selfridges, Totnes Wine, Whitebridge
Wines and Uncorked**). Find the merchant nearest you
and give them a ring. This is an astounding wine and it is
certainly one of the best Sauvignons that Isabel has ever
made. The nose jumps out of the glass, reeking of pungent
elderflower, lemon zest, melon, passion fruit and gooseberries.
The palate almost crackles with electricity as the tropical
flavours ripple across the tongue ending in a nervy, acidic,
thirst-quenching finish.

£9.99 **Cape Mentelle Sémillon/Sauvignon Blanc**,
2001, Margaret River, Western Australia, Australia (**Averys,
D. Byrne, Corks, General Wine, Handford, Harvey Nichols,
Charles Hennings, S.H. Jones, Odd, Peckham & Rye,
Philglas, Selfridges, Soho Wine, Tanners, Villeneuve, Wai
and Wimbledon**). Near perfection. The addition of 30%
barrel-fermented fruit fills out the mid-palate and makes
this wine blossom. The nose is typically luscious for
such a blend, with ripe tropical fruit and lime juice leaping
from the glass. The palate is richer than previous
vintages thanks to the stylish oaked part, and yet the finish
is as lively and refreshing as ever. Cape Mentelle is one
of the finest wineries in the world, and this wine will blow
you away.

LIGHT, DRY AND UNOAKED

£9.99 **Vergelegen Reserve Sauvignon Blanc**, 2001, Stellenbosch, South Africa (**Odd and Sai**). Vergelegen Farm has released one of the finest Sauvignon Blancs ever to be made in the Cape. The first-class grapes for this vibrant, vigorous 'reserve' wine are harvested three weeks later than those destined for their normal cuvée. The extra 'hang time' on the vine ensures optimum ripeness. Every Sauvignon Blanc hallmark can be found in this wine, rolled up into an amazing mouthful. Tease a tenner out of your wallets, and spend it wisely on an infusion of elderflower, lime, asparagus, gooseberry, flint, fig, pear, nettle, melon and racy acidity.

£11.00 **Geoff Weaver Lenswood Sauvignon Blanc**, 1999, Adelaide Hills, South Australia, Australia (**Ballantynes, H & H Bancroft, Philglas and Wimbledon**). The subtlety and complexity of this powerful, intense wine is remarkable. The grapes come from the magnificent Stafford Ridge Vineyard and exude gooseberry, lime and passion fruit flavours. This may be the best Aussie Sauvignon I have ever tasted. If you like Sancerre, you'll not believe what has hit you with this wine.

LIGHT, DRY AND UNOAKED

£5.29 **Viña Esmeralda, Torres**, 2000, Penedès, Spain (**Boo, Bot, Odd, Selfridges, Thr, Wimbledon and WRa**). This Muscat/Gewürztraminer blend continues to go from strength to strength. As each new vintage is released, the style seems to get drier and livelier. The wonderful, zesty acidity kicks in just as the palate starts to get tropically fruity. Esmeralda is a universally appealing style of wine, with round, ripe, almost exotic flavours and a refreshingly crisp finish. It also has a bargain price for such assured winemaking.

£5.99 **Neethlingshof Gewürztraminer**, 2000, Stellenbosch, South Africa (**Odd**). A real surprise for those of you who follow this highly aromatic grape. It certainly has the floral, lychee and rose petal aroma of a Gewürz, but the palate is a complete shock. Instead of the oily, rich, broad feel so often associated with Gewürz, this wine is crisp, clean and racy. Part of the problem with this grape variety is that it is very much an acquired taste, usually because of its pungency and unctuousness. So Neethlingshof have come up trumps with a real find for those who have been frightened off before.

£5.99 **Simon Gilbert Card Series Verdelho**, 2001, Mudgee, New South Wales, Australia (**Amps, Bentalls, Corks, deFINE, Peter Graham, Thos Peatling, Philglas, Lea & Sandeman and Wine Society**). Verdelho is most famous as the grape used for medium-dry Madeira. So what is it doing in Australia? One of Verdelho's commendable

AROMATIC

attributes is that it loves the heat and manages to hang on to its acidity well, when other varieties just taste flabby. Consequently, a number of Aussie estates manage to make pretty exciting versions of this rare grape, with Simon Gilbert's 2001 being my favourite. The aroma of pineapple chunk, pink grapefruit and cream soda is simply electrifying, and the flavour is topped off with a nerve-tinglingly crisp, lively finish. This is a superb wine that would be a treat with salads and starters, as well as Asian-influenced food.

£5.99 **Tesco Finest Alsace Gewürztraminer**, 1999, Alsace, France (**Tes**). Oh dear, this bottle looks like the Trumpton design department got hold of the label. You may even want to fabricate your own slipcover for fear of having to stare at this shocker on your dining room table. But maybe it will make you focus on the contents. The artistic *faux pas* cannot dampen the deliciously succulent, peachy, spicy, lychee and rose water-flavoured wine. It even has a crisp, dry finish to complete the picture. So there's a happy ending after all.

£5.99 **Tokay-Pinot Gris, Cave de Turckheim**, 1998, Alsace, France (**Bot, D. Byrne, Thr and WRa**). This wine settles back on its exuberant fruit and lets the grape variety do the talking. Tokay-Pinot Gris is a totally underrated grape, whose finest work is performed in the northern French region of Alsace. Halfway between pungent Gewürztraminer and aristocratic Riesling, Tokay uses restraint and sits on the fence when it comes to definitive character traits. Suffice to say that the spicy, edgy, tropical richness on the nose and honeyed, pear and citrus palate craves tricky dishes.

£5.99 **Villa Wolf Pinot Gris**, 2000, Pfalz, Germany (**Wai**). This wine is made by German wine genius, Ernst Loosen. He crafts heart-achingly beautiful Rieslings in the Mosel and sells them for top dollars. But he understands that our lives do not revolve around off-dry Germanic wines, so he zipped off to the warmer Pfalz region to make a more macho white from the intellectually stimulating Pinot Gris variety. There must be awards coming his way for label and bottle design, as they are stunning. Taste-wise, you have never drunk a German wine like it. The pear, almond, lime, ginger, honey and nectarine fruit is full, dry and, dare I say it, powerful, with a broad, rich palate and long finish. The fruit flavours are savoury and luscious at the same time. This wine will show you in a sip what is going on in the minds of Germany's top wine brains.

£5.99 **Wakefield Riesling, Clare Valley**, 2001, South Australia, Australia (**Odd**). The most fashionable grape of the moment is Riesling. At least it is in Australia, where they have realised that it can produce refreshing, challenging and foody wines. Harnessing the sumptuous lime, honey and crunchy apple fruit, Wakefield's version is intense, unoaked and self-assured. Use this wine to sort out any difficult-to-match dishes.

£6.49 **Santa Julia Reserve Viognier**, 2000, Mendoza, Argentina (**Wai**). There is some serious depth and richness in this Viognier. I suspect it comes from the 20% portion that spends six months in new French oak barrels. The classic nose of peach kernel and apricot is present, but the body and texture of this reserve wine are particularly noteworthy. The oaked fruit pads out the frame, without actually tasting oaky. Clever stuff, and great value.

£6.99 **Bernkasteler Graben Riesling Kabinett, Dr H. Thanisch – Erben Müller-Burggraef**, 1999, Mosel-Saar-Ruwer, Germany (**Tes**). This is the epitome of Mosel Riesling. The fragrance alone is breathtaking. Rhubarb, fresh flowers, elements of tropical fruit and a zippy, off-dry finish all conspire to capture your olfactory system and hold it to ransom until you agree to drink more classy German wine. You must agree, and this wine will surely convince you.

£6.99 **Leasingham Bin 7 Riesling**, 2001, Clare Valley, South Australia, Australia (**Saf and Wai**). The 2000 vintage was a stormer and the 2001 is even more extreme (I know, I was in the vineyards at harvest time). This wine is one of a handful of Clare Rieslings in my Top 250. They are such enjoyable wines, with class, complexity, food-matching skills and eminently affordable price tags. This wine is a classic lime juice, sherbet and crunchy pineapple chunk combo. The nose and palate carry these disparate themes to a refreshing, zesty finish.

AROMATIC

£7.99 **Château de Nâges, Cuvée Joseph Torrès**,
1999, Costières de Nîmes, France (**Odd**). A serious wine. It is
even a notch up on the tremendous 1998, which I thought
would be an impossible achievement. This special cuvée is
made from the venerable Rhône grape Roussanne. For an
Old World wine it has an exotic feel, with white peach,
nectarine and mango flavours nestling beneath the calm
exterior. In addition to these heady aromas and flavours,
Château de Nâges has a honeyed texture and a clean, fresh
finish. I have never tasted Roussanne like this under twenty
pounds, let alone eight, so give it a go. I think it is one of
the best white wines on the shelves today.

£7.99 **Redbank Sunday Morning Pinot Gris**, 2000,
Pyrenees, Victoria, Australia (**Corks, Charles Hennings and
Selfridges**). This Pinot Gris, from the Pyrenees, is nothing
short of wondrous. I love the idea of a Sunday morning
wine! But seriously, Pinot Gris is a benchmark foody white
grape, coping superbly with Chinese and Asian-fusion
cuisine. This example has a creamy palate with a touch of
honey and tropical fruit. With a little more texture than
Sauvignon, and a little less fragrance than Riesling, SMPG
gives way to a neat, crisply acidic satisfying finish. I like this
so much I have ordered a few bots for myself.

£8.49 **Villa Maria Reserve Riesling**, 2000, Hawkes Bay,
New Zealand (**Odd**). A heavyweight Riesling with serious
intensity and floral fruit. The palate is exotic and tropical,
with a long, incredibly dry finish. I suspect that it will age

AROMATIC

for ever, as the acidity is so perky. But to be on the safe side I think you should tackle it sooner rather than later, with big, creamy main course dishes, where the acidity will slice rapier-like through the sauce. This is a hedonistic style of wine that will separate the men from the boys. Riesling fans will go bonkers, others will be a bit scared.

£8.60 **Kràtos, Paestum Bianco, Luigi Maffini**, 2000, Campania, Italy (**Bibendum**). My goodness me, this is about as obscure as it gets, but Kràtos is a blinder. Made from Greco and Fiano (two superb white Italian grapes), the aroma and flavour are absolutely captivating. You will be riveted to the spot by the stone fruit and piercing acidity balanced exquisitely with the rich quince and greengage palate. I have never had a wine like this before and for those of you with a passion for pioneering new taste bud territory, this is a treat.

£8.95 **Domaine de Grangeon Viognier**, 2000, Coteaux de l'Ardèche, France (**La Vigneronne**). Christophe Reynouard used to work as a winemaker for Georges Vernay in Condrieu. Georges is a Viognier expert, in fact he makes some of the best and most expensive versions of this mind-blowing grape variety in the world. Christophe then went home to take over his family domaine in the Ardèche. Guess what? He now makes sensational Viognier and sells it for a reasonable price. So if you fancy apricot blossom, peach kernel and honeysuckle, followed by nutmeg and citrus fruit, this is where to find it. Do not miss this wine.

AROMATIC

£8.99 **Albariño, Lagar de Cervera, Rias Baixas**, 2000,
Galicia, Spain (**Corney & Barrow, Jeroboams, Lay &
Wheeler, Christopher Piper, Reid, Roberson, Selfridges,
Tanners and Villeneuve**). Albariño is one of Spain's greatest
and most fashionable white grapes, although there is not
much competition for this title. With a haunting aroma of
peach and apricot, a ripe, honeyed palate and crisp apple
finish, it is a truly accomplished wine. If you have never
tasted this variety before, imagine Dr Frankenstein getting
to work on Viognier for the nose, Riesling for the palate
and Ugni Blanc for the zippy little finish. It may seem like a
lot of money to gamble on a seemingly eclectic style, but I
think the odds are strongly in favour of you loving this
delicious wine.

£8.99 **Fairview Viognier**, 2001, Paarl, South Africa (**Great
Western, Odd, Sai and Wai**). What a beauty. I am normally
a bit sceptical when the enchanting grape Viognier gets a
bashing from oak barrels. But this wine has proved me
wrong. The opulent peach and hazelnut aroma, coupled
with the rich, round, ripe palate is sheer perfection. There is
a distinct whiff of burnt caramel on the nose signifying
some oak, but this only adds another dimension to an
otherwise succulent offering.

£9.99 **Gewürztraminer Prestige, Paul Zinck**, 2000,
Alsace, France (**Wimbledon**). Zinck is a hero of mine. When
Alsace Gewürz is good, it is very good and very expensive.
But this one is superb and a mere tenner – hurrah. Rose

petals, lychees, rhubarb compote and delicate, old-fashioned perfume can be found on the nose, with a smooth, creamy, sultry palate following on behind. The finish is dry, nutty and apricoty and sets the mid-palate richness off to a tee. This wine has only just arrived on the market, so if Wimbledon Wine is nowhere near you, then phone the agents SWIG on 020 7903 8311 and ask them for an updated list of stockists.

£9.99 **Nepenthe Riesling, Adelaide Hills**, 2000, South Australia, Australia (**OFW, Wai and Noel Young**). The spanking new vintage 2001 (due in around Christmas) from Nepenthe is set to continue their faultless run of Rieslings. Made in the relatively cool region of Adelaide Hills, Nepenthe Riesling is one of Australia's most elegant and impressive wines. It has a near-perfect aroma of lime juice, honey and fresh flowers, with a ripe juicy, tropical palate and a clean, dry, lingering finish. The overall result is an exceedingly beautiful wine that makes you feel on top of the world.

£9.99 **Petaluma Riesling, Clare Valley**, 1999, South Australia, Australia (**Odd and OFW**). Petaluma make one of the icon Rieslings of the entire wine world. The stunning lime juice and honey palate is balanced perfectly with the crisply acidic finish. I tasted the 1990 vintage recently and it was wonderfully developed without showing any signs of slowing down. This 1999 is a mere spring chicken in comparison, but it still leaves the famous Rieslings of Alsace

AROMATIC

standing in terms of value for money. You will gasp at the splendour of the tropical fruit complexity, and perhaps add the Clare Valley to your list of the world's great wine regions.

£9.99 **Yalumba Eden Valley Viognier**, 1999, South Australia, Australia (**Ballantynes, Carringtons, Odd, Thos Peatling, Philglas and Wai**). Not quite as exotically fruity as other Viogniers in this book, but its aroma is very interesting indeed. The pervading scents of white pepper and ginger are beguiling and the citrus fruit and peach palate is full and long. The 2000 vintage will be released as soon as the 1999 runs out. I predict this will be in December. The 2000 has a more peachy nose than the 1999, and that great white pepper thing is still there. Unique.

£10.49 **Pipers Brook Gewürztraminer**, 2000, Tasmania, Australia (**D. Byrne, Martinez and Noble Rot**). I am certain that this is Australia's finest Gewürz, although, I must admit, I can't think of many others. All of the classic hallmarks are here, including the lychee and rose petal nose and the exotic fruit palate. But what I like about this wine so much is the glacially cool, dry finish. It makes it a seriously pungent mouthful that tails off to the calmest of finishes. It really is quite beautiful.

£10.49 **Pipers Brook Pinot Gris**, 1999, Tasmania, Australia (**D. Byrne and Peckham & Rye**). Is Tasmania the closest thing to Alsace down under? This 1999 Pinot Gris from Tasmania is delicious. But the 2000 that follows it is restrained, aloof and a bit standoffish, not giving anything away. Maybe it is just a little shy. I tasted this wine in Feb '01 and then again in July '01 and it had already started to gain confidence. By Christmas I am certain it will be positively flirty, showing a full compliment of gorgeously exotic fruit and a zesty, perky finish.

£13.95 **Grosset Polish Hill Riesling**, 2001, Clare Valley, South Australia, Australia (**Direct Wines, Fortnum & Mason, Grog Blossom, Hedley Wright, Milton Sandford, Philglas and La Vigneronne**). Jeffrey Grosset is one of the greatest winemakers in the world. I do not say this lightly. In fact, I haven't ever written this statement about any winemaker before. I have been profoundly moved by Gaia (his spectacularly perfect, Cabernet-based red wine) and also by his Polish Hill Riesling. This is one wine that may run out quickly. But you can be sure that every reader has started their search at the same time – 4 October, publication date of this book. So if you have read this and feel dizzy with delight about having the chance to reserve a bottle of Polish Hill, don't delay, go for it. If not, there is always next year. Oh, the wine – it is sheer Riesling utopia.

£13.99 **Pinot Gris, Herrenweg, Domaine Zind-Humbrecht**, 1998, Alsace, France (**Bot and WRa**). There is nothing like a wine that stops you dead in your tracks. This Tokay-Pinot Gris from the mega-famous Zind-Humbrecht winery is so extraordinarily intense and perfumed it needs to be tackled in three sniffs, not just one.

AROMATIC

The fabulous, smooth tropical fruit is viscous and mouth-coating, with acres of peach, pear, spice and honey. This is a tremendous effort.

£14.95 **Scharzhofberger Riesling Kabinett, Egon Müller**, 1999, Mosel-Saar-Ruwer, Germany (**Wai**). This is possibly the greatest ever young, elegant, dry Riesling I have tasted from Germany. The 1999 vintage was a stormer, Egon is a hero of mine and the vineyard itself is a legend. So it all adds up to make a pretty amazing combination. If, however, you feel the need to go for Egon's Auslese style (much richer and fearfully young at present) it is a notch up in price, or a £45 notch in fact. At the princely sum of £60 a bottle, you'd better be a fan.

£3.99 **Currawong Creek Chardonnay**, 2000, South
Eastern Australia, Australia (**Wai**). Currawong Creek is
barely oaked, using staves, not barrels. The technique
imparts some flavour, but also costs a fraction of the price
of a barrel, so this is the reason that it can be sold so
inexpensively. It is a very good wine, with more than
respectable levels of honeyed pear and apple fruit, and a
good mid-palate followed by refreshing acidity. In fact, I
have tasted this wine four times just to check that I haven't
made an error. Yes, this really is £3.99 and yes, it really is a
great wine.

£4.99 **Agramont Barrel-Fermented Crianza Viura/
Chardonnay**, 2000, Navarra, Spain (**Sai**). 'Barrel-
fermented' always sounds clumsy, and in the past oaked
Spanish white wines tended to be oxidised, medicinal and
headachey. But times are changing and this is a pristine
example of just how spearminty and honeyed these wines
can be. Old stinky wood has been banished and is never to
return at Agramont, and for under a fiver you get a
complex mouthful of wine. Viura (otherwise known as
Macabeo) is a remarkably dull variety; however, it blends
well with Chardonnay and comes into its own in this
delicious wine.

£5.99 **Alamos Chardonnay**, 2000, Mendoza, Argentina
(**Bibendum, Maj, Odd and Unw**). An absolute stunner.
Magnificent. The feel is one of a top-notch Californian
Chardonnay; indeed, I tasted Alamos alongside a £30

OAKED

example and it held its head high. If you like classy oaked Chardonnay, and that means anyone who drinks serious white Burgundy as well as New World styles, you will be amazed at this wine. The packaging is exemplary, the bottle itself is made from the heaviest, most expensive glass and the label looks understated and alluring. I have a feeling that the price of this cosmic wine may rocket in subsequent vintages because it is woefully underpriced at present, but I am not complaining. Hire a van and load up.

£5.99 **Les Quatre Clochers Chardonnay**, 1999, Limoux, France (**Tes**). This wine is well worth hunting down as good Limoux Chardonnays are really beginning to rival the wines of the Mâconnais (Burgundy). Les Quatre Clochers is remarkably serious at a sub-six-pound price tag. The oak barrels, used to good effect, have imparted a more noticeable yeasty, lime juice feel than you might expect, and the Chardonnay fruit can handle it. It is fully ripe with pear and honey entwined around a vanilla and citrus core. Slip this in front of a Burgundy fan and see what they say.

£6.49 **Dominio de Montalvo Barrel-Fermented Viura**, 2000, Rioja, Spain (**Bot, D. Byrne and WRa**). No, this is not an old fashioned white Rioja. Far from it; the fruit is pristinely zesty and lemony, with clean vanilla and nut flavours and a sensational core of wild honey and pressed limes. This is a complex glass of wine, as every time you stick your hooter in there is another flavour to spot. Viura tends to be a dull variety but Campo Viejo, who own

OAKED

this label, know how to retain as much of the fruit and flavour potential as possible, before using the oak sensitively, rather than bashing it with a barrel.

£6.49 **Vergelegen Chardonnay**, 2000, Stellenbosch, South Africa (**Odd and Sai**). Head for this crystal-clear, icicle-sharp Chardonnay from Premier League estate Vergelegen. There is a superb, controlled lime juice and spicy oak core to this exceedingly competitively priced wine which shows a degree of flair rarely found in sub-tenner bottles. If you fancy a style that is riper than Chablis but cooler and more focussed than an Aussie Chardonnay, then this wine is just the ticket.

£7.95 **De Bortoli Gulf Station Chardonnay**, Yarra Valley, 2000, Victoria, Australia (**Philglas, Reid and R.S. Wines**). De Bortoli's Yarra Valley wines are all great. But their flagship label is expensive and in short supply, so Gulf Station, the 'second' label, is a much better bet. The fruit for this wine is harvested from their cool, classy Yarra Valley vineyards and then aged in oak barrels. The recipe is virtually the same as their grander wine. So what does it taste like? Yarra wines tend to be restrained and elegant and this Chardonnay will appeal to fans of white Burgundy, with a honeyed, floral nose and buttery fig and pear palate.

£7.99 **Beringer Fumé Blanc,** 1999, California, USA (**Maj and Odd**). I am not usually a keen 'oaked Sauvignon Blanc' man, as this delightful grape tends to be dominated by the

OAKED

barrel flavour rather than working with it. However, Beringer are masters when it comes to Fumé Blanc. Among the aromas and flavours you can detect in this wine are the spice, toast and vanilla of the French oak barrels, balanced beautifully with a smooth, creamy, fig, pear, fresh herb, pineapple, citrus and melon palate.

£7.99 **Brookland Valley Verse One Chardonnay**, 2000, Margaret River, Western Australia (**Odd**). Verse One is Brookland Valley's second label, but it is so good it could easily be their top wine. The good news is that it is six quid cheaper than their flagship Chardonnay. A praline cream nose is followed seamlessly by a honey, pear and apple compote centre – all suspended on an exceptionally smooth palate. There is an awful lot going on here, so you have to concentrate or you'll miss something. This is a benchmark roast chicken or sea bass wine. Yum.

£7.99 **Castello della Sala Chardonnay, Antinori**, 2000, Umbria, Italy (**Maj, Unw, Valvona & Crolla and Wai**). A seriously well-made wine. Antinori are one of Italy's oldest wine families and here they have cleverly put their own Umbrian stamp on Chardonnay while subjecting it to subtle oak treatment. The result is a herby, zesty wine with honey, cream and almond flavours nestling beneath a citrusy Italian veneer. Castello comes from the same stable as the fabulous, but expensive, super-white, Cervaro della Sala. Castello, the baby brother, is a veritable bargain and borrows some of its sibling's skill and charm.

OAKED

£7.99 **Jordan Chardonnay**, 2000, Stellenbosch, South Africa (**Connollys, General Wine, George Hill, Jeroboams, Christopher Piper, Frank Stainton, Unw, Wai, Whitebridge Wines and Noel Young**). Pound for pound this wine gives every bottle of Chardonnay worldwide (and that's a few) a run for their money. Succulent peach and vanilla aroma, totally balanced fruit and acidity and an incredibly long finish are but a few of its hallmarks. Buy it and see!

£7.99 **Sigalas Vareli**, 2000, Santorini, Greece (**Odd**). When I first encountered this wine, the intense, golden, oily, oaky richness completely bowled me over. It has a quirky liquorice and honey core that expands on the palate, annihilating anything in its path. Is it the best white Greek wine on the shelves? Yeah, why not? Match it to assertive dishes as the acidity is commanding and the palate weighty.

£7.99 **Tim Adams Sémillon**, 1998, Clare Valley, South Australia, Australia (**Bot, Tes and WRa**). Year after year this wine is nothing short of sensational. I tasted the 1991 and 1992 recently and they were golden in colour, magnificent in structure, zesty in acidity and fascinatingly complex on the palate. The 1998 is intensely lime-juicy and almost oily in texture. The oak is present but not too dominant. I believe that this is quite simply one of the best dry Sémillons in the entire wine world, and at eight quid, it is a stupendous bargain. If you are feeling adventurous, buy a few bottles to stick in the cellar. You will be amazed with the results.

OAKED

£8.52 **Saint-Véran, Bernard Morey**, 1999, Burgundy, France (**Domaine Direct**). Bernard Morey is a meticulous and talented winemaker based in the renowned village of Chassagne-Montrachet. Hilary Gibbs of Domaine Direct asked him to make a Saint-Véran for her, as the majority of Saint-Vérans are a little bit lean and green. He agreed, and here it is; and there is no way you would say that this is a Saint-Véran in any respect apart from the price. Bernard seems to have made a mini-Chassagne, so if he can do it, other people are clearly not trying hard enough! Top Chardonnay from Burgundy under a tenner – no, not a typing error.

£8.93 **Rosemount Hill of Gold Chardonnay**, 2000, Mudgee, New South Wales, Australia (**Asda**). This pretty New World Chardonnay is almost neon green in colour, and after one mouthful the bright, taut, citrusy fruit careers around your palate. It has a long finish that is so mouth-watering you just can't resist taking a sip every few minutes in order to keep the flavour going. The freshness of the fruit and the tangyness of the oak are enormously uplifting. If you have had a hard day at work, a chilled glass of this is the vinous equivalent of a top-to-toe massage, followed by a jump into an icy plunge pool.

£8.99 **Delegat's Reserve Chardonnay**, 2000, Hawkes Bay, New Zealand (**Maj, WCe and Saf**). A rich, sophisticated, creamy and completely over-the-top Chardonnay from one of the best-known estates in New

OAKED

Zealand. I tend to veer towards carefully oaked wines, favouring balance and elegance over pure muscle. But this wine has reminded me of how delicious and uninhibited big, sexy Chardonnays can be. If, like me, you have been wandering around in unoaked or moderately oaked territory recently, then tear yourself away and come back for one fabulous bottle – this one.

£9.99 **Boekenhoutskloof Sémillon**, 2000, Franschhoek, South Africa (**Peter Graham, Martinez and Odd**). I have some shocking news for those of you who were lucky enough to get hold of the 1999 vintage of this wine. You will not believe this, but the 2000 is even better. Now get up off the floor and read on! Mark Kent is the genius, alchemist winemaker behind Boekenhoutskloof and he is already setting world benchmarks with their wines. There is also a Cabernet and a Shiraz in the stable, so grab them if you see them. Sadly, they are in much shorter supply than this jaw-droppingly serious, hundred-year-old-vine Sémillon. I have decided to avoid writing tasting notes for this wine for fear of causing my readers repetitive superlative injury, suffice to say that it is a star.

£9.99 **Bourgogne Blanc, Clos du Loyse, Château des Jacques, Louis Jadot**, 1999, Burgundy, France (**Arthur Rackham and Wimbledon**). I know that this wine sits in the oaked section of the book, but when you open the bottle you will wonder why, as the fruit and oak are in perfect balance. It has a rather unexciting label, as do all

OAKED

Jadot wines, but once you have the wine in your glass, you
will be rewarded with crisp, luscious apple and pear-scented
Chardonnay fruit, with a whisper of hazelnut and vanilla ●
and a seamless finish. This is a classy wine for white
Burgundy lovers on a budget.

£9.99 **Errázuriz Wild Ferment Chardonnay**, 2000,
Casablanca Valley, Chile (**Amps, Odd and Sai**). 'Wild
Ferment', phew, what a sexy name for a wine. This wine
would not sound half as tempting if it were labelled
'Natural Ferment' or 'Non-inoculated Ferment'. The idea is
not a new one; the grape juice is allowed to ferment using
naturally occurring yeasts as opposed to the more common
practice of using shop-bought versions. This wild decision
results in a remarkably restrained, classy wine, with
flavours such as pear, vanilla and butterscotch mingling
with crème brûlée, lime and freshly baked patisserie. More
educated than wild, wouldn't you say?

£10.99 **Hautes-Côtes de Beaune, Bois de Messé,
Rijckaert**, 1999, Burgundy, France (**Odd**). Classy white
Burgundy at just over a tenner – sounds good? Well this
wine is a well-crafted beast indeed. The controlled
oak and rich, honeyed fruit are in perfect balance. Rijckaert
is a new name to me, but I will be keeping a close eye on
him from now on. White Burgundy is such a foody wine
I would save this bottle for a special occasion. It would
certainly do justice to any dish, but if you asked me to
choose just one, it would have to be roast chicken.

OAKED

£10.99 **Vasse Felix Sémillon**, 1999, Margaret River, Western Australia, Australia (**Handford, Lay & Wheeler, Christopher Piper and Noel Young**). This stunning wine is intensely lime-juicy with pineapple chunk and mouth-watering lemon-sherbet fruit, gently overlaid with vanilla toast oak nuances. It spends only four months in French and American oak barrels, but this is enough to give the wine a lick of resin and a tangy finish. The green/gold-coloured wine ages like clockwork, as most Sémillons do. But my advice is to tackle it in its youth (the extra perky new 2000 will be available at Christmas) when the tart, taut citrus fruit is at its most cheek-sucking.

£11.95 **Cullen Sauvignon Blanc/Sémillon**, 2000, Margaret River, Western Australia, Australia (**Adnams**). Vanya Cullen is a star. She has a fantastic talent for building into each and every one of her wines complexity and layers of fruit that seem to evade everyone else. Part of the trick with this wine is to blend 70% new oak barrel-fermented Sauvignon Blanc with 30% stainless steel-fermented Sémillon. This seems about face to me as Sémillon usually handles oak better than Sauvignon, but it just shows you why I write about wine rather than make it, because the result is earth-shatteringly spectacular. Every wine from this estate is a revelation.

£12.99 **Prelude Chardonnay, Leeuwin Estate**, 2000, Margaret River, Western Australia, Australia (**Domaine Direct, Harvey Nichols and Selfridges**). Leeuwin Estate Art

OAKED

Series Chardonnay is one of the most profound Aussie white wines. It is my favourite New World Chardonnay. And there is a lot of competition for that title. Prelude is Leeuwin's second label and it is very much a chip off the old block. Superb control, elegance and fruit complexity shows just how amazing the Garden of Eden conditions in Margaret River are. This wine is stunningly oaked and exceptionally long. Barely drinking, it will live for three or four years easily, so try to exercise some self-control. This is the best Prelude to date.

£12.99 **Vavasour Single Vineyard Sauvignon Blanc**, 1999, Marlborough, New Zealand (**Peter Graham, Martinez, OFW and WineTime**). This magnificent Sauvignon Blanc comes from the famous McBride vineyard in Marlborough. It is one of the oldest vineyards in the region, and year after year yields superb fruit. Some 40% of Vavasour Single Vineyard Sauvignon Blanc is aged in new French oak barrels for four months. During this time it picks up depth, weight and texture. It is unlike any other Kiwi Sauvignon in that it has very un-Sauvignon weight and presence, but a classic nose and flavour. The other interesting fact is that winemaker Glen Thomas holds this wine back so that it cannot be drunk too young. Epic.

£13.99 **Esk Valley Reserve Chardonnay**, 1998, Hawkes Bay, New Zealand (**Peckham & Rye, Roberts & Speight and Wimbledon**). A big Chardonnay, but by no means top heavy. This wine is balanced from the spicy, honey-laden,

OAKED

toasted brioche nose all of the way to the last lingering flavour of mandarin and crème brûlée on the palate. The oak is starting to give way as the wine enters its second phase of life, but it has years ahead of it, as the sheer structure is astounding. If you like buxom Chardonnays, this wine will keep you happy for hours.

£14.19 **St. Aubin, 1er Cru En Remilly, Château de Puligny**, 1999, Burgundy, France (**Bibendum**). When white Burgundy fulfils its pre-release hype it is a complete result. This wine lives up to its importer's claims to be one of the best value, serious white Burgundies around. The grapes come from a vineyard just a few yards from the monster Grand Cru, Chevalier-Montrachet. The wine is rich and ripe, with toasty oak and a full bodied, honeyed Chardonnay palate. It is drinking well already but will continue to develop for a further four or five years. I love it.

£14.99 **Ravenswood Lane Beginning Chardonnay**, 1999, Adelaide Hills, South Australia, Australia (**Amps**). It is no surprise that Philip Amp dived in here when he tasted this. He has an astute palate and is the first UK retailer for this cosmic wine. But, between me finishing this book and it being published, I can guarantee that other merchants will follow Philip's wise lead. Capricorn Wines (0161 908 1300) are the UK agents, so phone them for stockists. Beginning is fine, balanced, generous, classy and rich. The cool Adelaide Hills region is a top venue for awesome Chardonnays. This is Meursault from Australia.

OAKED

£14.99 **Wakefield St Andrews Chardonnay**, 1998, Clare Valley, South Australia, Australia (**Evertons, Charles Hennings, Laithwaites, Playford Ros, Raeburn, Roberts & Speight, Saf and Wimbledon**). It is seemingly sacrilegious to grow Chardonnay in the Clare Valley, as it is such hallowed Shiraz and Riesling turf. But when something is as good as this, you ignore all the rules and just go for it. This is a diva of a wine. Huge fruit, busty, teetering along on tiny heels. The rich, honeyed exotic flavours, coupled with the sweet, smoky oak nose all add up to a real star performer.

£16.95 **Planeta Chardonnay**, 1999, Sicily, Italy (**La Réserve, Valvona & Crolla, Wai and Wimbledon**). Heavenly. This wine has scooped the *tre bicchieri* award in the latest edition of the Gambero Rosso, which means that it is one of the best wines in Italy. I wouldn't stop there. This is one of the best Chardonnays in the world. It kicks most top Californian efforts into touch and is more elegant than many top-end Aussie versions. Stratospheric.

£5.95 **Château Grande Cassagne, Rosé**, 2000, Costières de Nîmes, France (**Gunson, Haslemere Cellar and La Vigneronne**). Grenache and Syrah combine to make this beautiful rosé which bursts with crushed raspberry fruit and has a refreshing, bone-dry finish. It is food-friendly, and can be drunk with starters, Indian and Chinese food, even seafood. Served a touch warmer than fridge-cold, it takes on red wine characteristics and can match chicken, pork, cold roast beef, ham salad and charcuterie.

OAKED

£2.79 **Domaine de Richard, Vin de Pays de l'Aude**,
2000, Southern France, France (**Maj**). It doesn't get any
cheaper than this. £2.79, minus the duty, the margin,
the shipping and the VAT, leaves very little money left for
the wine. I calculate about 32 pence in fact, and we haven't
costed in the bottle, cork, label and capsule! So it is
remarkable that this wine is so good. The Grenache/
Carignan blend is juicy, balanced and accurate and, if
you're having a party, there is no question – just buy it.
Oh, if your name is Richard you can always pretend you've
had it specially made for you!

£3.99 **AlmuRan Monastrell**, 2000, Alicante, Spain (**M&S**).
Monastrell is the Spanish name for the grape variety
Mourvèdre. Telmo Rodríguez, the inspired winemaker
behind this wine, strips away some of the rustic elements
of what is a rather coarse grape and polishes the remainder
into a bright plum and cherry winner. It is a lovely little
mover that will work with a wide variety of dishes and is
drinking perfectly now. What a result for only £3.99.

£3.99 **Banrock Station Shiraz/Mataro**, 2001, South
Australia, Australia (**Coo, Mor, Saf, Sai, Som, Tes, Unw and
Wai**). Well, well, a delicious, inexpensive wine that is also
available in a bag-in-box (£14.99 for 3 litres) and still tastes
great! Make sure you buy this blend of Shiraz and Mataro
(Mourvèdre), as it is an awesome, spicy, densely briary,
smooth-textured wine packed with jammy, black fruit and
blackjack aniseed-scented character.

LIGHT AND FRUITY

£3.99 **Il Padrino Rosso**, 2000, Sicily, Italy (**Odd**). What a superb price for this compact Italian sportster. Spice, liquorice, a whiff of rosemary, blackberry jelly and bitter cherry sweeties, the tang of dark chocolate and the trademark mouthwatering Italian acidity are the exact order in which the smells and flavours bombard your senses. What's more, the bottle looks every bit Italian – with a minimalist, chic label and a catchy and, thank goodness, pronounceable name. You can't go wrong. Watch out for this stylish bottle clogging up every bottle bank in the country.

£3.99 **Nero d'Avola/Syrah Firriato**, 2000, Sicily, Italy (**Wai**). Some 85% Nero d'Avola is tweaked with 15% Syrah to make this fun-packed Sicilian red. It is spicy, juicy and easy-drinking. The purity of fruit is amazing at this price. The Waitrose team sourced the brew themselves, knowing exactly what flavours make their customers happy. You could happily drink it with any of your winey friends and they would have no idea that the wine cost a mere £3.99.

£3.99 **Seriti Pinotage**, 2000, Western Cape, South Africa (**Boo, Inspired Wines and Noble Rot**). This baby Pinotage is a veritable pocket-rocket. Even at this lowly price, the winemaker has skilfully managed to capture the essence of the variety. Juicy, black fruit flavours mingle with spice and fresh herbs. This is a classic emergency red that should be kept by the caseload, under the stairs, in case of unexpected guests, or impromptu parties. Light enough to be a glugger,

it can also handle simple chicken and meat dishes. In
addition, it has the benefit of a smart label design, so all in
all this wine is a winner. I have no doubt that it will be in
even wider circulation by the time this book is published,
so keep your eyes peeled.

£5.49 **Valpolicella Classico Superiore, Masi**, 1999,
Veneto, Italy (**Odd**). Masi's Valpol looks superb. Its black
and white label is so striking I'm sure people pluck it off the
shelf for sheer pose value. Thank goodness the contents are
up to it as well. This wine is fairly mellow and juicy
compared to many other Valpolicellas. The bitter cherry
fruit doesn't get in the way too much and it's a real crowd-
pleaser. So why do I like it so much? Because sometimes
you have to chill out, slow down and unhook your brain
from the wine thing. You need a wine that is not too
taxing, but presses all the right buttons. This is it.

£5.99 **Beaujolais-Villages, Combe aux Jacques**,
2000, Burgundy, France (**Asd, Hoults, Saf, Tes, Wai and
Wimbledon**). This is the definitive version of Beaujolais-
Villages for those who have long since given up on the
region, thanks to the banana-scented, headache-inducing
alcopop masquerading as Beaujolais Nouveau. The French
have finally decided that we, in the UK, shouldn't have to
put up with the Nouveau sham every November, so instead
buy this superb, dark purple, blackberry-steeped wine. It is
the perfect foil to food and there is not a wine-drinking
human alive who will not appreciate its class and charm.

LIGHT AND FRUITY

£5.99 **Simon Gilbert Card Series Shiraz**, 2000, Mudgee, New South Wales, Australia (**Amps, Bentalls, Corks, deFINE, Peter Graham, Thos Peatling, Philglas, Lea & Sandeman and Wine Society**). 'Aussie Beaujolais' and 'super glugger' were two tasting notes I made about this wine. But how can Australian Shiraz be 'light and fruity'? Well, Simon Gilbert, with twenty-eight years' experience making wine, knows that not all red wines should be built like Arnie. The stunningly designed Card Series is made for no nonsense, early drinking. There is no oak getting in the way, just pure, unadulterated pepper and berry fruit. As the super 1999 gives way to the fresh, lively 2000, I, for one, will be hosing down a few bottles with friends.

£6.99 **Morgon, Georges Duboeuf**, 2000, Beaujolais, France (**Sai, Tes and Unw**). There is nothing airy-fairy about this 'cru' Beaujolais from the village of Morgon. It is a meatier offering than, say, a Beaujolais-Villages, with its cherry-scented fruit and its focussed structure. It has the ability to age gracefully for two or three years, despite drinking well now. Of the ten important villages in Beaujolais, Morgon is a favourite of mine. Georges Duboeuf is probably one of the best-known French winemakers in the world and this wine is one of the most multi-skilled when being matched to food.

£7.70 **Chiroubles, Domaine de la Grosse Pierre**, 2000, Beaujolais, France (**Haynes, Hanson & Clark**). I love top flight Beaujolais, and Alain Passot, who makes this wine, is a mastercraftsman. The Gamay grape variety is in superb shape in this 2000 Chiroubles. Bright garnet colour, lively red fruit nose and succulent, plump palate tail off to a dry, clean, tannin-less finish. This wine can be served ever-so-slightly chilled to elevate the nose and focus the perfume, or at room temperature to expose the earthier elements, making it darker, meatier and more robust.

£7.99 **Ninth Island Pinot Noir**, 2000, Tasmania, Australia (**Booths and Noble Rot**). Light and fruity wines are not always inexpensive. This pure, strawberry fruit Pinot Noir, made by Dr Andrew Pirie of Pipers Brook, is a case in point. However, followers of Pinot know that this grape doesn't get into its stride below this price, so as a relatively inexpensive New World Pinot, Ninth Island is a joy. It is light enough in body to handle fish and chicken dishes, and even to drink on its own. It is a totally yummy wine that will not test you, just charm you.

£3.99 **Caño, Viña Bajoz** , 2000, Toro, Spain (**Bibendum and Evertons**). This Garnacha has only just been shipped into the country, so telephone Bibendum Wine, the agents, to get details of more stockists, because it is so brilliant it is destined to be sold everywhere. Pure, earthy, plummy, liquorice fruit, with a superb mouth-filling texture, all beautifully packaged and sold for a minuscule price. This wine behaves like a much grander beast and I am certain that in a year's time, most wine drinkers will know the name well. Caño means dawg, pooch or mut, so you must make up your own slang for this Scooby of a wine. You heard about it here first.

£4.49 **Santa Julia Bonarda/Sangiovese**, 2000, Mendoza, Argentina (**Mor, Saf and Wai**). Chunky Bonarda and spicy, leathery Sangiovese are a natural double act. They fit together like puzzle pieces and for that simple reason, Santa Julia works incredibly well. This is a fruit-driven, stocky little red with charm, spice and a teeny price. It is a Friday-night-staying-in-and-watching-telly wine.

£4.49 **Segada, Trincadeira Preta/Castelão Frances**, 2000, Ribatejo, Portugal (**Bot, D. Byrne, Odd, Sai, Thr, Unw, Waterloo Wine and WRa**). Segada is a taste collision between a home-made summer pudding, a blackberry gobstopper and crispy duck with hoisin sauce. It is gamey, plummy and yummy with a volcanic eruption of fruit flavours in its juicy core. I have never encountered such exuberance before in a wine without it tasting sweet.

MEDIUM WEIGHT

It will shock you and your friends and you can play 'search for the flavour', as almost anything you can think of is here. This is a bargain of a wine, that surely points the way for the future of Portuguese winemaking. Oh, and chilled, it goes so well with Chinese food!

£4.99 **Argento Malbec**, 2001, Mendoza, Argentina (**Asd, Bibendum, Bot, Coo, Maj, Saf, Sai, Som, Tes, Thr, WCe and WRa**). A spicy, dense, black-fruit cocktail that is even richer than Argento's impressive 2000 vintage. The 2001 has slightly more texture and intensity and yet continues to stay true to the Malbec variety with an earthy twist running down its backbone. It is hard to see how this much fruit and intensity can be sold for less than a fiver, but it is, and I am certainly not complaining. Match this with any meaty dish, from sausages and mash to fillet steak, and you'll be delighted with the result.

£4.99 **Carneby Liggle, Old Bush Vine Red**, 2001, Western Cape, South Africa (**Asd**). This wine is as weird as it gets. The blend of grapes in this funky brew is as follows – 40% Shiraz, 40% Zinfandel and 20% Cinsault. The question was, how would the South African Wine Board allow such a blend of disparate bedfellows? Could this be legal? The wine scraped through after a tussle and the jazzy name Carneby Liggle, or 'couldn't be legal', was born. Taste-wise this is a meaty, juicy wine with overtones of strawberry liquorice, blueberries and plums. Just the sort of wine to warm up your palate on a wintry day.

MEDIUM WEIGHT

£4.99 **Canaletto Primitivo**, 2000, Puglia, Italy (**Peckham & Rye, Peter Graham, Roberts & Speight, Springfield, Charles Steevenson, Villeneuve and The Wine Cellar**). A few Primitivos have crept into the Top 250, so what is different about this one? Well, it is one of the least expensive for a start, it is juicy and forward and is already drinking very well unlike the 'A Mano', for instance, which is more structured and could last a year or so. And it is the only one that works well when chilled a touch. When cool, the purple, vivacious palate and spicy, plummy nose really come alive. So if you are having chilli-flavoured food, whether it is con carne, on a pizza, Mexican or whatever, this is the thirst-quenching wine to go for.

£4.99 **Conde de Navasqüés Tinto**, 1998, Navarra, Spain (**Asd**). This is one of the smartest sub-fiver Spanish reds around, and there is a rumour that Asda may discount it to £3.99 for a promotion, so keep your eyes peeled. Made from Garnacha and Tempranillo, this wine is plump, rich, opulent and cherry-scented. If you like Spanish reds, with their juicy red fruit and vanilla-perfumed oak nuances, this wine is spot on. It is perfect for wintry dishes, particularly if you are having a party, when you can be happy that you are serving a top-flight wine, and saving a few quid in the process.

£4.99 **Inycon Aglianico**, 2000, Sicily, Italy (**Sai**). Aglianico is a superb grape variety to glug alongside spare ribs, crispy duck, oriental meaty dishes, chargrilled steak and burgers! It is juicy, with coffee, liquorice, plum and blackberry flavours

MEDIUM WEIGHT

leading the way on the nose and palate. The finish is soooo smooth and soooo long, you'll not only be delighted at the value for money, but also, before you know it, you will have added yet another grape variety to your repertoire.

£4.99 **Natural State Montepulciano**, 2000, Marche, Italy (**Wai**). The Montepulciano grape usually underwhelms me, but this is a star. It is sourced from fifteen- to fifty-year-old organically farmed vines, and then half of the batch is put into posh French oak barrels to mature. The result is a much richer, foodier wine than expected, with cherry and blackberry fruit in abundance and a savoury, dry finish. The fact that it sits under the fiver mark only serves to heighten my excitement about this super little pocket Ferrari.

£4.99 **Norton Sangiovese**, 1999, Mendoza, Argentina (**Odd and WCe**). Sangiovese is the Chianti grape. But Chianti at a fiver is torture as usually only the leftovers make it into the bottle. So further afield, several thousand miles away in Argentina, where the sun shines and the grapes are happy, Sangiovese has got to be a good bet. It is. In fact it is a very good idea as this fruity wine shows. There are even leather notes and the fresh herb thing that fine Chianti engenders. So if you are always losing out on a famous style of wine, change the rules and think outside the box. It is worth it.

£4.99 **Primi**, 2000, Rioja, Spain (**Bibendum, Som and Tes**). A Rioja under a fiver? It had to happen one day, but who would have thought that it would be this good? Made from two

MEDIUM WEIGHT

grand Spanish red grapes, Tempranillo and Garnacha, Primi differs from most Riojas because it has not seen the inside of a barrel. But I don't think this makes any difference to the impact of this plummy and cherry-flavoured wine. It is smooth, tangy and rich and, for less than a fiver, quite brilliant. I confidently predict that you will see this wine everywhere when the snowball effect starts to gather momentum.

£5.49 **Accademia del Sole Carignan Família Zarrouk**, 2000, Tunisia (**Bibendum and Sai**). This is the best of a recent influx of North African wines to hit the shelves. Brian Fletcher (Fletch), lately of Evans & Tate in Western Australia, makes this beauty. Here, the hairy beast (the grape Carignan, not Brian, although…) is stripped of its belligerent blunt, charmless attributes and transformed into a superb, sweet, juicily intense, black fruit-soaked babe. Brian cleverly remembers to weave in some earthy, spicy notes, just to give the wine quirkiness and balance.

£5.49 **Altano**, 1999, Douro, Portugal (**Brian Coad, Corney & Barrow and Wai**). They have cracked it. The famous Symington port house has come up with a juicy, inexpensive red wine that looks great and tastes fab. Their porty grape varieties are used here to create a black-fruit-driven, medium weight wine with superb acidity, which will find a place on the dining tables of discerning chefs around the country. This is because the acidity cuts neatly through fleshier (cooked pink) meat dishes such as lamb, veal or pork, without overshadowing the intricacies of the cooking.

MEDIUM WEIGHT

£5.49 **Deakin Estate Shiraz**, 2000, Victoria, Australia
(**Odd**). The explosion of pepper and blackberry is well
judged on this budget beauty. There are a million Aussie
Shirazs on the market and Deakin's is not the biggest,
juiciest or most structured. It is, however, the sort of wine
that will appeal if you like Crozes-Hermitage or other
northern Rhône reds. The colour is purple, the nose spot on
and the palate expressive, but not cooked or overly
alcoholic. This is an everyday style of wine at an affordable
price that will keep your bank account in the black and your
palate smugly satisfied.

£5.59 **Deakin Estate Merlot**, 2000, Victoria, Australia
(**Odd and Wai**). Deakin's family of wines is always priced
around a fiver, and as Merlot rarely performs admirably at
lower price points, this was always a wine to watch. Bingo,
they have cracked it again (that's now three years in a
row). Plummy, with savoury spice and cranberry fruit, a
warming palate and a hearty finish, mean that while this
is a hearty, wintry, juicy red wine, it is also easy to glug.

£5.99 **Alamos Malbec**, 2000, Mendoza, Argentina
(**Bibendum, Maj and Tes**). This wine is the older, more
serious, multi-talented brother of Argento Malbec. The
main difference between the two is the addition of some
very sexy oak barrels and even more succulent, sultry black
fruit. I wrote 'mega' in my tasting notes and the fact that
it sells for only a pound more than the Argento makes this
a must buy. A monumental achievement.

MEDIUM WEIGHT

downright delicious

£5.99 **A Mano Primitivo**, 2000, Puglia, Italy (**Balls Brothers, Bennetts, Ben Ellis, Butlers, Boo, deFINE, Edward Sheldon, Great Gaddesden, Martinez, Noble Rot, The Old Forge, Philglas, Playford Ros, Sai, Shaws, Sommelier Wine, Valvona & Crolla, Villeneuve, Wines of Interest, Winesmith and Noel Young**). The 1999 release of A Mano coincided with the arrival of a flurry of equally juicy, robust and flavour-packed Primitivos. But I suspect that the 2000 vintage will see A Mano distancing itself from some of its competitors. The intensity and complexity of the liquorice and blackberry palate is downright delicious. This wine also has a fair degree of grip to the back palate, guaranteeing a smooth ageing period over the next two years. A dead cert with most meaty and cheesy dishes, and pizza and pasta.

£5.99 **Barbera d'Asti, Fiulot, Prunotto**, 2000, Piedmont, Italy (**Maj and Valvona & Crolla**). It is rare to find accurate Barberas these days. They either tend to be gutless and dull, or souped up and overblown, like a kit car with too many spoilers. This version is, however, authentic, and great value. Here the juicy, plummy Barbera grape makes a bright purple wine offering a whiff of summer pudding and a tangy, tart finish. It likes occasionally to be chilled a touch for hot and spicy food, or served at normal temperature for cheese and more carnivorous dishes.

£5.99 **Barrington Estate, Pencil Pine Chambourcin**, 2000, Hunter Valley, New South Wales, Australia (**Asd**). I love this wine. Every time I open a bottle, my guests go

MEDIUM WEIGHT

nuts, and cannot believe the value for money. It is one of the all time classic wines to have with crispy duck. Made from the unusual and rarely sighted Chambourcin grape, the nose is intense and berry-drenched. The palate is velvety smooth with roasted coffee bean, sweet wood, blackberry, plum and blueberry all lining up to be enjoyed. Find this beauty – you are guaranteed to love it, too.

£5.99 **Cairanne, Domaine de l'Ameillaud**, 2000, Côtes-du-Rhône-Villages, France (**Unw**). You'll be amazed when you uncork this Grenache, Syrah, Carignan and Mourvèdre blend. It is a mini-Châteauneuf-du-Pape in every respect. The price tag is minuscule, but the flavour is commanding. The peppery, spicy nose and black fruit-drenched palate are a joy. Give it a quick decant to air the wine before drinking. Its ideal partner is leg of lamb, but if you are partial to cheese, Keen's Cheddar would be my choice.

£5.95 **Château Grande Cassagne, La Civette**, 2000, Costières de Nîmes, France (**Gunson, Haslemere Cellar and La Vigneronne**). If you want to buy a 'house' wine for the festive season, or you are expecting a rugby team around for Sunday lunch, then this is the wine for you. Civette is a Grenache/Syrah blend, expertly assembled by the incredible team at Grande Cassagne. The rich blackberry-infused nose is boosted by bonfire and pepper mill nuances. The palate is fully ripe and plump with great texture and viscosity. The finish is grippy and dry, calling out for food, be it beef, lamb, roast turkey or a plate of farmhouse Cheddar.

MEDIUM WEIGHT

£5.99 **Elderton Tantalus Shiraz/Cabernet**, 1999, Southeast Australia, Australia (**Berry Bros. and Odd**). More accustomed to sniffing out Old World gems, this is a strange wine to buy from Berry Bros. on St James's Street in London. But if you want to taste it, then at least buy your first bottle there because the seventeenth-century shop is unforgettable. This wine is made by the Shiraz-kings Elderton. Tantalus sounds tantalising, and indeed it is. Not a heavyweight, but a superbly balanced wine, with pepper, black cherry and charred oak all mingling together on the palate. You must get in quick, as this wine will move fast.

£5.99 **Errázuriz Merlot/Cabernet Sauvignon**, 2000, Rapel Valley, Chile (**Wimbledon**). Imagine a world where inexpensive red Bordeaux was juicy, rich, ready to drink, a fiver and reliable. Stop, it doesn't exist, all right! So if you need your Bordeaux-blend hit, at a realistic price, where do you go? Chile, of course, and in particular Errázuriz who are past masters at handling these two grapes. This wine is plush, stylish and balanced. It exudes ripe blackcurrant fruit and a long finish. You will never have to worry about Bordeaux again.

£5.99 **Graham Beck, Coastal Merlot**, 2000, Coastal Region, South Africa (**Bibendum, Sai, Wai and Noel Young**). This newly released wine, from the accomplished cellars of Graham Beck, is a delight. I love full-on Merlot, especially when the flavours are as pure and fruit-driven as they are in this glorious wine. It is superb, with smooth, plummy, fruitcakey fruit, topped off with a haunting scent of smoky oak. There is an awful lot of wine in this bottle for the money and it should send a warning shot across the bows of the Californian wine industry, who seem incapable of releasing a Merlot under a tenner that is half as good as this.

£5.99 **Miranda, Rovalley Ridge Petit Verdot**, 2000, South Australia, Australia (**Tes**). Petit Verdot is rarely bottled on its own. In fact, it usually only plays a minor role in a blend. This is because it is a bitter little fellow that struggles to ripen fully – its name means 'little green one'. But you can always rely on the Australian sun to do its thing and Miranda is a fabulous opportunity to experience the majesty of this variety. Blackberry juice is the main theme, with smoky oak and a burnt, herbal, almost Italian element lurking beneath the superbly intense chassis.

£5.99 **Top Garnacha, Bodegas Borsao**, 2000, Campo de Borja, Spain (**Bibendum**). I would put money on this wine being sold in enormous quantities in the supermarkets, but my tasting sample arrived a long way ahead of the first shipments, so you will have to ring Bibendum to find out where to look. As the name suggests, this red is made from the top batch of young Garnacha vines at the high-tech Borsao estate. The sweetness of berry fruit and depth of tangy, herbal flavour is superb. The length on the palate is staggering, and if you have yet to be wowed by the vast improvements made by the Spanish wine scene in the last decade, this wine will surely convince you.

MEDIUM WEIGHT

£5.99 **Villa Tonino Nero d'Avola, Baglio Curatolo**, 2000, Sicily, Italy (**Liberty, Philglas and Valvona & Crolla**). This is the GTI version Nero d'Avola from Tonino. And it is a feisty little fella. Made from one of the best indigenous red Sicilian grapes, this special cuvée is smoky, spicy, rich and plummy, with an awful lot more power than you'd expect at this price. I always get a coffee/mocha note on Nero d'Avola and this wine is no exception. It is the sort of red wine that you can mellow out with after a big dinner.

£5.99 **Wakefield Promised Land Shiraz/Cabernet**, 2000, South Australia, Australia (**Bacchanalia, D. Byrne, Evertons, Hoults, Mor, Odd, Terry Platt, Raeburn, Saf, Som, Wimbledon and Wright**). A budget bruiser stuffed with lusciously sweet black grapes. The six months they spend soaking up aroma and flavour in American and French oak barrels is just enough to augment the overall taste, rather than dominate it. The resulting concoction is balanced and drinking very well despite its relative youth. This is a harmonious wine that would complement a range of meaty and cheesy dishes.

£6.49 **MontGras Carmenère Reserva**, 2000, Colchagua Valley, Chile (**Sai, Valvona & Crolla, Wai and Wimbledon**). MontGras was one of the first top-flight Carmenères to hit the market a few years ago. Since then, winemakers have been dividing up their vineyards into Merlot and Carmenère plots rather than lumping it all in together and calling it Merlot – good news, as the varieties are noticeably

MEDIUM WEIGHT

different. The plum and roasted coffee bean nose holds the sweet vanilla and oak scent well and opens the palate out to a broad, lusciously exotic berry flavour. This is a hell of a lot of wine for the money. Watch out for mega-MontGras super-cuvée Ninquén '99 (£20) hitting the shelves soon.

£6.99 **Beringer Zinfandel**, 1998, California, USA (**Maj and Odd**). Spot on! Neither too heavy and lumpy, nor too light and confected, this well-priced Zin is fabulously juicy and briary with just the right amount of spice. It is interesting that Beringer, an old stalwart estate, is still one of the most reliable names on the Californian scene. Other wines come and go, but Beringer just keeps its head down and concentrates on the job in hand – making good wine. If you haven't had a Zin before, start here and you'll be hooked.

£6.99 **Bleasdale, Mulberry Tree Cabernet Sauvignon, Langhorne Creek**, 1999, South Australia, Australia (**Odd**). Mulberry Tree is a very useful wine indeed. It is guaranteed a massive fan base because it has all of the fleshy blackcurrant and black cherry fruit that you would expect from an Aussie Cabernet, with none of the breathy, heady alcohol or plodding, soupy framework. There is a ton of flavour here, but it is in perfect balance with the spicy, savoury oak and fresh PYO berry notes. The purple, inky colour and bright, juicy nose are seamlessly woven into a shiny, lustrous body with a refreshing finish. Served a touch chilled, this wine will mesmerise your senses, without emptying your wallet.

MEDIUM WEIGHT

£6.99 **Fairview Merlot**, 2000, Coastal Region, South Africa (**Maj**). Plump, plummy and Simon Templar smooth, this Merlot is juiciness itself, seasoned with a brief spell in two- and three-year-old barrels. The barrel aroma is manifested in the briefest of vanilla-scented kisses, which in turn give way to blueberry, redcurrant and mint flavours sauntering across your tongue. Can you tell that I like this wine a lot?

£6.99 **Fairview Zinfandel/Cinsault**, 2000, Paarl, South Africa (**Odd**). This funny old blend actually tastes more Zin-like than it does Cinsault-y, which is a good thing really as Cinsault can be a bit of a brute. Spicy, plummy Zin is blended with blackberry and earthy Cinsault and the combo is a winner. It has great style with bright purple, glossy fruit and a juicy fruit-driven palate. Although it is dead young, this wine is ready to drink now. It will warm you up on a chilly evening.

£6.99 **MontGras Quatro**, 1999, Colchagua Valley, Chile (**WCe and Wimbledon**). MontGras have come up trumps with their Quatro, as Audi did with theirs. Quatro impeccably combines four (hence the name) super-sexy red grapes. Cabernet Sauvignon, Merlot, Carmenère and Malbec are represented proportionally on the label by a four-colour design. This successful blend aims to bring balance and complexity to the table in the form of a harmonious, luscious, plum, blackberry and loganberry cocktail, seasoned with a liberal dunking in some classy French oak barrels. What a result.

MEDIUM WEIGHT

£7.99 **Barón de Ley, Reserva**, 1997, Rioja, Spain (**Asd, Bot, Thr and WRa**). Old-fashioned Rioja can be a bit stewed, oaky and dried out. However, some estates continue to favour the oakier, vanilla and raspberry style and it can work. Barón de Ley is a case in point, and when you taste this classic wine you may yearn for a return to the old days. Rioja is an icon wine and, with the producers split between traditionalists and modernists, it is nice to see one of the members happy and successful in what they do. There will be an Asda promotion at some stage when this wine will be reduced to £5.49 – be vigilant.

£7.99 **Brookland Valley Verse One Cabernet/ Merlot**, Margaret River, 1999, Western Australia, Australia (**Odd**). Verse One is Brookland Valley's second label. This classic blend of Cab and Merlot is superbly judged, with a smattering of oak and a large dollop of Ribena-drenched juice. It is ready to go – no ageing is needed. It will delight fans of these two famous varieties and, like Graham Beck's Coastal Merlot, should inspire the Californians to try harder to make wines as good as these below ten pounds. If you have plans to grill a steak in the near future, then don't attempt it without this wine.

£7.99 **Coldstream Hills, Briarston**, 1998, Yarra Valley, Victoria, Australia (**Odd**). For some unknown reason, Briarston is priced at £7.99, when the rest of the top-end Coldstream Hills wines are over fifteen quid. I am a huge fan of this Bordeaux blend (Cab Sauv/Cab Franc, Merlot and

MEDIUM WEIGHT

a teeny bit of Malbec), as it is fabulously intense without being too heavy and alcoholic. The Yarra Valley is a little cooler than many Aussie regions and the elegance of fruit is evident here. Claret fans will adore this wine, as it is rare to find red Bordeaux under a tenner that is even remotely palatable – apart from in this book, of course!

£8.50 **Vega Lara, Crianza**, 1997, Ribera del Duero, Spain (**M&S**). Ribera del Duero is Spain's most trendy micro-region. The wines that emerge are usually ballistically priced, awesomely concentrated, impenetrably tannic and need to hide in a cellar for a least a decade before you dare to wave a corkscrew in their direction. But this fella is affordable drinking and seriously attractive. The sweet oak nose and red fruit palate, coupled with unmistakable Ribera classiness, give this wine a degree of flair and breeding that far outshines its price tag.

£8.95 **Château du Maine, Graves**, 1998, Bordeaux, France (**Lea & Sandeman**). I am usually so rude about 'inexpensive' red Bordeaux. The most disappointing tastings of the year are the young red Bordeaux marathons. Teeth-staining tannin, unripe fruit, high acidity, old-stinky-barrel flavours. Yuk. So when I tasted this wine I nearly keeled over. It is brilliant. If I sound surprised then sorry, but it is brilliant. Plump, fresh, juicy, blackcurranty; and a whiff of sexy oak barrels swirls around in the glass. This is the sort of wine that attempts to set the record straight. I wish there were more. Until that day, keep this one to yourself.

MEDIUM WEIGHT

hypnotise your *taste buds*

£8.95 **Rosso di Montepulciano, Villa Sant'Anna**, 1999, Tuscany, Italy (**Lea & Sandeman**). The boys at Lea & Sandeman really know how to buy Italian wine. This Tuscan star is made from Sangiovese, the Chianti grape. It has a deep purple colour and a perfect nose of black cherry, rosemary and dark chocolate. Italian reds often have a healthy kick of acidity on the finish that can dent their appeal somewhat. This wine is super-smooth. The velvety fruit is so well balanced, it makes this a totally engaging wine. It will hypnotise your taste buds in seconds – you'll be booking a holiday in Tuscany before you know it.

£8.95 **Viña Salceda, Crianza**, 1998, Rioja, Spain (**Averys, Balls Brothers, Berry Bros., Haslemere Cellar, George Hill, Goedhuis, S.H. Jones, Lea & Sandeman, Portland, R.S. Wines, Tanners and Wine Society**). This Rioja is so even, harmonious and red cherry fruit-infused, it is a delight. I have been following Salceda for five or so years and they are never overpriced and always, despite the vintages, make great wine. I prefer their Crianza to their pricier Reserva and Gran Reserva as it is more expressive and fruity. There is a touch of oak, but other than that the palate is pure strawberry, raspberry, cherry and vanilla-drenched. A superb wine with roast lamb or Christmas dinner.

£8.99 **Château Bournac, Cru Bourgeois, Médoc**, 1999, Bordeaux, France (**M&S**). The great thing about this wine is that it is only two years old, but is drinking perfectly. It is so boring to have to hang around for

MEDIUM WEIGHT

inexpensive red Bordeaux to soften, particularly when Cabernet/Merlot blends from the rest of the world have already kicked off. But this one is ready to go. Made from 60% Cab and 40% Merlot and poshed up in a third new oak barrels, Château Bournac is remarkably concentrated, succulent and blackcurrant. This is the way forward for Sunday lunches! Claret lovers can relax at last.

£8.99 **Jordan Cabernet Sauvignon**, 1998, Stellenbosch, South Africa (**Connollys, General Wine, Jeroboams, Christopher Piper, Frank Stainton, Unw and Wai**). A truly succulent cassis brew from one of the master-wineries of the Cape. Jordan's entire portfolio is a result (see White Oaked) and they are all remarkably well priced. You get an awful lot of 'bang for your buck' here and, along with the cassis body, there is class, complexity, cedarwood and vanilla. The palate is dreamy, with a super-smooth finish.

£8.99 **La Segreta Rosso, Planeta**, 2000, Sicily, Italy (**La Réserve, Valvona & Crolla and Wimbledon**). This hedonistic brew, a blend of Nero d'Avola, Merlot and Cabernet Sauvignon, is made by the trailblazing team at Planeta, Sicily's leading winemakers. With high-tech wineries and some breathtakingly situated vineyards, Planeta's wines have catapulted to the top of discerning wine lovers' shopping lists. Erudite, swaggering Diego, the father of the clan, is unremitting in his quest for global recognition. Segreta Rosso is rich, smooth, chocolatey and succulent with scents of blackberry, plum and roasted coffee beans.

£8.99 **Wither Hills Pinot Noir**, 2000, Marlborough, New Zealand (**Great Western, Odd, Edward Sheldon, T & W, Wai and Wine Society**). Another stunner from magician Brent Marris. This is one of the coolest Pinots on the planet. It is less than a tenner, but packed to the gunwales with strawberry and lovely sweet oak. Brent used 70% new oak barrels for this wine and it really works, complementing the intense fruit and driving the wine forwards. I scored it eighteen out of twenty – a score usually reserved for wines ten times this price. I am placing my order for a few bottles and will uncork them with roast chicken and chips.

£9.95 **Morellino di Scansano, Le Pupille**, 2000, Tuscany, Italy (**Amps, Bennetts, deFINE, Peter Graham, Valvona & Crolla, Villeneuve and Noel Young**). This is the best-ever vintage at Le Pupille and the fruit used for this wine could easily have gone into the Riserva label (£20). But here we are with a superb chance to secure some awesome wine before the Americans fleece the estate. This is basically a super-charged Chianti-style with nobs on, from an area in the south of Tuscany (halfway between Pisa and Rome). You do not need a tasting note, just get on the phone.

£9.99 **Nebbiolo d'Alba Occhetti, Prunotto**, 1998, Piedmont, Italy (**Odd**). No Barolos have made it into my Top 250. Are you surprised? I'm not. They are always too expensive and unbelievably tannic. With all of that sinewy, terrifying Nebbiolo crammed into a barrel, what do you expect? But what about this wine, with its enticing price

MEDIUM WEIGHT

point and delusions of grandeur? It is made from the same grape as Barolo, comes from the same place, it is even made by a Barolo producer, but this time the wine is juicy, fleshy, deep, spicy and plummy, with refreshing tannins, not enamel-stripping ones. Hurrah for this cheat-Barolo, it gives you what you want, when you want it, at a fair price!

£10.49 **Ramsay Pinot Noir, Lot 14**, 1999, California, USA (**Odd**). Californian Pinot Noir is always expensive. This is a fact. Don't buy a cheap one, it is not worth it. Sadly, this has passed the psychological tenner barrier, but it is still one of the best Pinots on the market. It has more 'oomph' than many New World examples yet will keep a Burgundy fan happy. Plum and black cherry, a juicy mid-palate, and wild strawberry aromas make this one of the best tenners (OK, just over) you'll spend on a bottle of Californian wine.

£10.99 **Château d'Agassac, Cru Bourgeois, Haut-Médoc**, 1998, Bordeaux, France (**Saf**). This is classic, old-fashioned claret. And it is worth the dosh. A touch young at present, but nothing that half an hour in a decanter wouldn't cure, its blackcurrant fruit, robust backbone and great depth of flavour is totally balanced with a cigar-box-and-pencil-lead aroma. Sunday lunch wine.

£13.95 **Whalehaven Pinot Noir**, 1998, Hermanus, South Africa (**Amps, D. Byrne, deFINE, Peter Graham, Handford, Philglas, Lea & Sandeman, La Vigneronne, Wright and Noel Young**). Whalehaven is the brainchild of Strom Kreusch, the former winemaker of the mega-serious Hamilton Russell Estate, producers of South Africa's leading Pinot Noir. She has moved on to set up a winery that is already catapulting her into international Pinot stardom. This wine is an eclectic brew (Pinot-philes love eclectic wines), using fruit sourced from Elgin and Walker Bay – two cool areas yielding top-flight grapes. The resulting wine is sensational, and despite its pale colour, has a wonderful aroma and flavour of wild strawberries. Those of you who are into Pinot Noir must track this down.

£13.99 **Veenwouden Merlot**, 1998, Paarl, South Africa (**D. Byrne, Andrew Chapman, Grog Blossom, Handford, Hedley Wright, S.H. Jones, Martinez, La Réserve, Sommelier and Noel Young**) If you are a Bordeaux fan, in particular the wines from the Right Bank areas of St-Emilion and Pomerol, then this wine is for you. After having worked in the region at Château Bon Pasteur, winemaker Marcel van der Walt seems to have picked up a few tricks. This is even a wine that could teach the French a thing or two. It is instantly expressive, with layers of dense, juicy red and black fruit. The liberal dunking in French oak has lent this wine an aristocratic air, something you would not get from a fourteen-pound claret.

£16.50 **Barratt Pinot Noir**, 1999, Piccadilly Valley, Adelaide Hills, South Australia, Australia (**H & H Bancroft and Philglas**). A perfect Pinot Noir nose of wild strawberries and cherries is followed by an exquisitely balanced, lengthy

MEDIUM WEIGHT

palate showing all of the hallmarks of a period of time spent in French oak barrels. I gave this wine nineteen plus, out of twenty, when I first tasted it in Australia. I never give out scores like that, what was I doing? So I tasted it again back at home in Sandwich. Yup, it's a great wine. Nothing gets twenty, so this has to be a nineteen! If Bannockburn equals Vosne, then Barratt equals Volnay (Burgundy bores unite!).

£16.95 **Marqués de Vargas, Reserva**, 1997, Rioja, Spain (**Adnams, Berry Bros., Direct Wine Shipments, El Vino, Handford, Haslemere Cellar, S.H. Jones, Lea & Sandeman, Thomas Panton, Portland, La Réserve, Laurence Smith, Tanners and Weavers**). At a recent Rioja tasting that I was hosting, this wine shone above all others. There are bigger, more imposing wines out there, but for sheer splendour and romance this is sensational. It has so many layers of red and black fruit, oak and vanilla, they seem to unravel on the nose and palate as you work your way through the bottle.

£17.99 **Bannockburn Pinot Noir, Geelong**, 1999, Victoria, Australia (**Ballantynes, Bennetts, Carringtons, OFW, Philglas and Tanners**). This is one of the finest Aussie Pinots I have ever tasted and it is due on the shelves in December. Granted it is not cheap, but if you were to search for this kind of black cherry intensity in red Burgundy you'd be throwing a lot more money at a bottle. What sets Bannockburn aside from the rest is the mouth-feel. The viscosity and depth of this wine is tremendous, without ever appearing cumbersome. Mind-blowing.

£5.97 **Xanadu, Secession Shiraz/Cabernet**, 2000, Western Australia, Australia (**Asd, Odd and Som**). Everything about this brew is impressive – the deep purple colour, the stunning, pure Ribena and spice nose, the classy, long, punchy-plum finish. Xanadu is a great winery and this wine is surprisingly inexpensive. I have followed Secession for a few years now and it has always been a winner. This red blend is one of the most cosmic wines around. Reliable, intensely juicy, elegantly packaged and a bargain; you cannot say that very often these days.

£5.99 **Finca El Retiro Malbec**, 2000, Mendoza, Argentina (**Bennetts, House of Townend, Frank Stainton, Valvona & Crolla, Wai and Noel Young**). These guys hit the ground running in 1998. I have followed each vintage since and they simply get better every year. They take the earthy, blunt, often-stewed grape Malbec and turn it into a gorgeously extracted, purple, blackberry-scented beauty. There is power here, so don't just open this after work for a glass. Plan the evening carefully. For a start, turn the oven on, because food is needed with this imposing wine. I would err on the side of meaty. But cheesy is fine – better still, pasta with a hefty sauce. Mmmm.

£6.99 **Santa Julia Reserva Tempranillo**, 1999, Mendoza, Argentina (**Asd and Unw**). This reserva Tempranillo is a knee-trembler of a wine. With creamy, smooth blackberry and vanilla flavours that saunter on to your palate, and a long, juicy, plump finish, this is a succulent, full-bodied

BLOCKBUSTER

red 137

version of this meaty grape variety. Tempranillo is usually
found propping up the lion's share of the blend in Spain's
most famous red wine, Rioja, but it just goes to show how
well some sturdy grape varieties travel.

£7.49 **Clos Petite Bellane, Valréas**, 2000, Southern
Rhône, France (**Odd**). The newly released family of 2000s
from Clos Petite Bellane is amazing. It starts with a useful
Côtes-du-Rhône (£5.99), then my featured Valréas, a
Vieilles Vignes (£7.99) and finally Les Echalas (£8.99). They
are all brilliant, but I have decided to focus on the Valréas
because it is meaty, spicy and densely fruity, but also ready
to drink. The VV and Echalas each need a spell in the cellar,
but don't half represent incredibly good value for money.
But what is it about these wines that has completely
knocked me sideways? They all have an intense nose of
wild blackberries and ground pepper, followed by a
luxurious palate constructed of the ultimate in red and
black fruit maceration, soaked in freshly cut timber and
nestling beneath a Balkan Sobraine tobacco haze.

£7.99 **Carmen Reserve Carmenère/Cabernet
Sauvignon**, 1999, Maipo Valley, Chile (**Berry Bros., Odd
and WCe**). This wine is deep, dark and brooding, although
the tannins are not overly hard. What is remarkable about
it is the nose that the Carmenère gives to the robust
Cabernet. It is spicy, blackcurranty and has a distinctive
whiff of pipe tobacco. And, despite not favouring a pipe
myself, it is a very pleasant aroma indeed.

£7.99 Chianti Classico, Villa Cafaggio, 1999, Tuscany, Italy (**Ballantynes, Berry Bros., D. Byrne, Sandhams, Unw and Woodhouse**). The entire range of Cafaggio wines is exceptional. My recommended wine is at the bottom of the ladder of labels, but it still packs a punch. The intense black fruit, herbal twang, leathery scent and bitter cherry finish make for a classic. It will be approaching its peak at Christmas and will hold for a further three or four years. So this is definitely one wine to buy a few bottles of. I am delighted that top Chianti Classico remains such great value. It is one of the noble wines of Italy. San Martino and Cortaccia are this wine's big brothers. They are even more extracted and impressive, but they do cost a bit extra!

£7.99 Domaine Borie de Maurel, La Féline, 1999, Minervois, Languedoc, France (**Odd**). This wine comes from the outstanding Borie de Maurel stable. Each and every wine they make is a winner. Féline is made from the perfect southern French cocktail of grapes – 70% Syrah, 20% Grenache, 10% Carignan. It is a feisty red, which is just about drinking and would love to spend some time with a wintry stew or similarly meaty dish. The dense, spicy, blackberry fruit is sensational. It is a great price for this enormity of power and complexity, and if you like Rhône reds you will love this. Aussie winemakers should look closely at this style of wine and its value for money. Many of their red wine prices are drifting skywards, and there are but a handful of eight-pound Aussie reds that have the complexity and integrity that this wine offers.

BLOCKBUSTER

red 139

£7.99 **Errázuriz Syrah**, 2000, Aconcagua Valley, Chile (**Wai**). An outstanding effort from expert estate Errázuriz. The intense, stunning nose and palate of blackberries and freshly ground pepper is seasoned with toasty, smoky oak. There is a 'reserve' Syrah that sells for two pounds more, but I reckon that this wine is more attractive, more forward and has better balance. The reserve is oakier and more tannic and will not really be ready for a further two years. So save a few quid and unlock the tremendous aroma, seductive flavour and minutes-long finish of this epic wine. Class.

£7.99 **Hollick Shiraz/Cabernet**, 1999, Coonawarra, South Australia, Australia (**Balls Brothers, Hedley Wright, R.S. Wines and T & W**) I have tasted Ian Hollick's 2000 vintage of this wine as well as the 1999, just in case the 1999 runs out after you read this. Both wines are, of course, fantastic. The reason that they may move quickly is because of their sheer value for money. When I first encountered this terrific wine in Australia (the '98) I somehow noted the price down incorrectly. On my return to the UK I tracked it down to buy for a restaurant in London. When I ordered it, my wine waiters and I were amazed. I had assumed that it would be twice the price. So, well done Ian, this stunning intense, fleshy, juicy, smooth, savoury wine is a bargain.

£7.99 **Peter Lehmann Shiraz**, 1999, Barossa Valley, South Australia, Australia (**Odd, Saf, Sai, Wai and WCe**). This Shiraz is sitting in here because it is more of a blockbuster

than a medium weight red. Peter Lehmann's definitive
Barossa Shiraz is a burnt, purple, black fruit-soaked
mouthful with a whisper of seaweed and pepper. It is a real
man's wine. The structure is sturdy and the nose almost
sneeze-inducing because of the pepper element. I adore this
real old-style Aussie wine. There has been no focus group
honing this wine's flavour, no lifestyle guru diluting its
message and no modernist whippersnapper tweaking its
recipe. Just Peter and his team's desire to be true to their
beloved Barossa Valley. Drink this true brew with meat.

£7.99 **Redbank, Fighting Flat Shiraz**, 1999, Pyrenees,
Victoria, Australia (**Carringtons, Corks, Charles Hennings,
Thos Peatling, Peckham & Rye, Selfridges and Noel Young**).
Fighting Flat has a rich, blackberry and plum-dunked-Shiraz
feel. It is made by the terrific estate Redbank, whose top
wine, Sally's Paddock, would cost you a tenner more. But
for my money, this wine looks far better value. The great
thing is that while Sally's needs cellaring, Fighting Flat
comes out fighting. The nose alone is a knockout and the
palate is briary, spicy and succulent.

£7.99 **Les Romains, Les Domaines Camplazens**,
1998, Vin de Pays d'Oc, France (**M&S**). From La Clape, in
the south of France, this Cabernet Sauvignon, Merlot,
Grenache, Syrah, Carignan blend is nothing short of
spectacular. It is very much a 'drink it and weep wine'.
Romains is everything you should expect from the
magnificent 1998 vintage, coupled with inspired winemaking

BLOCKBUSTER

and lovely packaging. Despite being a few years old – this wine could live happily for a further five – it is thrilling, with immense presence and buckets of rich, dense, black fruit topped with stunningly well-balanced, oaky nuances.

£7.99 **Q Tempranillo**, 1999, Mendoza, Argentina (**Bot, Tes, Thr and WRa**). From the first glimpse of the wonderful designer bottle, to the last molecule of liquid dancing a footloose-flavour tango on your tongue, this wine is absolutely astonishing. The often dowdy, stewed-tasting Rioja grape, Tempranillo, has been given a fantastic makeover, probably by the vinous equivalent of Lawrence L-B. With eye-catching design, completely over-the-top fruit bursting out everywhere, acres of purple velvety juice and a highly textured palate, this wine really makes a scene. Lush, almost sweet, ripe raspberry and vanilla fruitiness accompany this sensory bombardment.

£8.99 **Evans & Tate, Margaret River Shiraz**, 2000, Western Australia, Australia (**Grog Blossom, Hedley Wright, Hoults, Irvine Robertson, Oxford Wine Co., Philglas, Portland, Saf, Winchcombe and Wright**). Good Lord, for a supposedly cool region this wine doesn't half chuck out some fruit. Briary, warm and spicy, with an extremely juicy palate of blackberry fruit and burnt smoky oak, this is an ogre of a brew. There is an awful lot of wine here (a magnum's worth in flavour alone) for the price, so put your crash helmet on and arm yourself with a corkscrew. Once more unto the breach etc.

BLOCKBUSTER

£8.99 **Fairview Cyril Back Reserve Shiraz**, 1999, Paarl, South Africa (**Wai**). Black in colour and intensely rich on the palate, this is a monster wine. Shiraz is fast becoming one of South Africa's strong suits. It is a wonder that this size of wine can be sold for such a reasonable price. The mega-concentration means that it should be reserved for those of you with iron stomachs and a desire for huge Henry VIII-style banquets. Put your seatbelt on!

£9.99 **Canale Estate Reserve Merlot**, 2000, Rio Negro, Argentina (**M&S**). This is the only wine in my Top 250 that is seriously young and not yet ready to drink. So why put it in? I suspect that over the course of the next year, some of you will want to buy a present for a wine-loving friend. This can be a daunting task, particularly if they already have a decent collection of wine. But I can assure you they will not have heard of this explosive, intense Merlot from the arid Rio Negro Valley. The nose is juicily ballistic and the palate is impenetrably tannic. All that is needed is a few years slumbering in a cellar to make this wine a work of art. While I'm on the subject of presents, you could give your pals this book!

£9.99 **Neil Ellis Cabernet Sauvignon**, 1998, Stellenbosch, South Africa (**Asd**). Neil Ellis has a careful touch when it comes to oak barrels. The temptation to lock this immaculately conditioned Cabernet fruit away for eighteen months in smart barrels must have been unbearable. But he didn't. Instead the wine shows the same results that food

BLOCKBUSTER

does when it has been seasoned correctly. The flavours are all allowed to speak in turn, and perfect balance is achieved. This is a superb wine, with a suave cassis core surrounded by an array of perfectly tailored oak and spice nuances.

£9.99 **Rosemount Hill of Gold Cabernet Sauvignon**, 1999, Mudgee, New South Wales, Australia (**Wai**). Having spent eighteen months in French and American oak barrels, this dense, purple, blackcurrant-infested Cabernet from Rosemount's prime-sited Mudgee vineyards could really do with a spell snoozing in a wine rack for a year or two. But you can drink it now, just make sure you have a hefty plate of food in front of you. Better still, decant this bruiser and let it relax for a few hours, then you'll smell and taste its unrestrained excellence.

£9.99 **Rothbury Estate Brokenback Shiraz**, 1999, Hunter Valley, New South Wales, Australia (**Odd**). It is time to get very serious indeed. This spicy, dense Shiraz from the Lower Hunter Valley, positively steeped in black cherry fruit, is a beast of a wine, relishing the chance to be let out of its cage. The vines used are low yielding; the result is an imposing wine with an intensely fruity, velvety body, trimmed with gorgeously seductive oaky nuances. This is one of the grandest sub-tenner reds of the season.

£9.99 **Saxenburg Private Collection Shiraz**, 1998, Stellenbosch, South Africa (**Berry Bros. and Odd**). In South Africa this is regarded as one of the top Shirazs around. It is

BLOCKBUSTER

also very expensive. Over here it is dear, but not overly so, and few people have heard of it. So it's about time I formally introduced you to Saxenburg PC. This purple, inky wine is monstrously concentrated, but controlled in terms of weight on the palate. The nose gives the impression that you are in for a basting, but in fact PC has harmonious blackberry, plum and pepper fruit and a seriously long finish. This Jekyll and Hyde wine is stupendous.

£9.99 **Tim Adams Fergus**, 1999, Clare Valley, Australia (**Australian Wine Club and Maj**). Fergus is a legend. I have drunk every vintage of this wine since it hit our shores last century. Grenache-based, but with a smattering of other varieties, this is a spicy, herbal, plummy and bright purple concoction. It is vibrant and punchy, with a black fruit core, good acidity and grip, and yet can be drunk a mere two years into its life. Grenache never seems to hog the spotlight in the same way as Shiraz does, but Fergus is set to change that. All you have to do is buy it. The wine is named after the Fergus and Vyv Mahon who own the vineyard from which this majestic wine is made.

£9.99 **Veramonte Primus**, 1998, Alto de Casablanca, Chile (**Bentalls**). If you do not live near Bentalls in Kingston-upon-Thames then ring the UK agents Stokes on 020 8944 5979 and they may have some new stockists for you. Primus is made from 85% Carmenère and 15% Cabernet Sauvignon. It is a noble wine, with a calm, smooth, classy chassis and a rich, deep, chocolate and plum centre. The nose has the trademark sweet oak, coffee and tobacco scent that you'd expect, and the finish is long. This wine is right up there at the top of the pile of Chilean reds.

£9.99 **Wynns 'Black Label' Cabernet Sauvignon**, 1997, Coonawarra, South Australia, Australia (**Bot, Direct Wines, Maj, Odd and Thr**). This is one of the most famous and significant Aussie red wines. It epitomises the relationship between soil and grape variety. The Cabernet used is grown on the terra rossa (red earth) of Coonawarra, one of the most important stretches of dirt in the southern hemisphere. A standard-bearer for excellence, Wynns always manage to pack Black Label with cassis, mint, eucalyptus and oak. The 1997 is drinking beautifully now; complete, classic and fully ripe. The 1998, due to arrive soon, is even bigger, but more of a backward beast, with a longer life ahead of it.

£9.99 **Yalumba Mawson's, Coonawarra**, 1998, South Australia, Australia (**Ballantynes, Carringtons, Odd and Thos Peatling**). Mawson's, named after Sir Douglas Mawson, an intrepid Australian explorer, adventurer and all-round hero, is a clever wine. The rich, spicy, structured grapes Cabernet Sauvignon and Shiraz (63% and 31% respectively), from prime Coonawarra turf, have been blended with a dribble of Merlot (6%) to create a classy, almost elegant red wine. The blend was matured in French and American oak barrels giving a degree of sweetness and complexity. This wine is a worthy homage to a great man.

BLOCKBUSTER

£11.99 **Chianti Classico, Fonterutoli**, 1999, Tuscany, Italy (**Valvona & Crolla, Wimbledon and Wine Society**). The Mazzei brothers know exactly what they are doing. And that is redesigning the image of Chianti at home and abroad, by making astoundingly assured wines. The fruit texture and aroma engendered by their wines is almost sensual. At the risk of sounding like an old fruit I'll stop there. I find it incredibly exciting when a wine pushes back the boundaries of an established region, but that is what this Chianti Classico is doing. It is New Worldy in feel, yet authentic in flavour, accessible despite its youth, yet will undoubtedly age like clockwork. I can't get enough of this fabulous wine.

£11.99 **Tyrrells Rufus Stone Heathcote Shiraz**, 1999, Victoria, Australia (**Odd**). I am a huge fan of Rufus Stone Shiraz. But when I tasted Rufus's Heathcote (three pounds more than the straight RSS), I was floored. But why should you trade up from a brilliant £9 wine to this £12 bottle? Because Heathcote displays the fundamental intensity and purity of the noble Shiraz grape. This is not a big, sweaty, over-alcoholic, medicinal style; it has a wonderful smooth texture with coffee and mocha tones mingling with the pepper, warm leather and black fruit elements. What sets this wine apart from a lot of top-end Aussie reds is the charm, depth and complexity of flavour. There is none of the brash, brazen, pumped-up, baked fruit that finds its way into other super-cuvées, just faultless, exquisite balance with a magnificent finish.

£12.29 **Torres Cordillera**, 2000, Curicó Valley, Chile (**Ameys, Corney & Barrow, Peckham & Rye and Helen Verdcourt**). This wine is made from very old vines – 60% Cariñena, 30% Syrah and the remaining 10% being Merlot. Despite its youth, Torres Cordillera is awesomely exuberant and hurls out concentrated, velvety flavours of chocolate, blackcurrants and plums. The wine was aged for a relatively short period in oak barrels, resulting in a tobacco leaf, roasted coffee bean and vanilla pod scent. Chilean wine is great value at the fiver mark, but when trading up few wines have really hit the spot. This wine, however, has scored a bull's eye.

£12.49 **Julio's Vine Cabernet Sauvignon, Barrelli Creek Vineyard**, 1996, Sonoma County, California, USA (**Tes**). This magnificent thoroughbred comes from the famous Gallo stable in California. It is a huge, juicy, brooding monster of a wine with a thick, glossy black coat wrapped around a mouthful of intensely ripe blackcurrant and spice flavours. It provides a great opportunity to try a fairly mature wine which, at five years old, is drinking perfectly. Make sure that you decant this wine so that it has a chance to unwind, and a heavenly bouquet will emanate from the decanter. With Julio's Vine Cabernet Sauvignon, Gina Gallo (Julio's granddaughter) has achieved her goal in making a truly amazing wine that, despite its seemingly lofty price tag, can compete with any of the micro-boutique, ultra-hyped Napa Valley Cabernets that sell for upwards of fifty quid.

£12.99 **Starvedog Lane Cabernet Sauvignon**, 1998, Adelaide Hills, South Australia, Australia (**Amps, D. Byrne, Jeroboam, Noble Rot, Sommelier and Noel Young**). The UK agents, Capricorn Wines on 0161 908 1300, secured one listing for this wine a month before it had even hit our shores in July! 'Starvers' Cab is a sleek, black limo of a wine. It is smooth, luxurious and impeccably balanced with gloriously controlled oak and plump, brooding, blackcurrant fruit. A whiff of leather and spice and a long mellow finish complete the picture. Five star enjoyment all round.

£13.99 **Renwood, Old Vine Zinfandel**, 1999, Amador County, California, USA (**Odd**). It was a joyous day when the first Renwood shipment arrived in the UK. The 1998 Old Vine was one of my favourite all-time Zins. However, the 1999 seems to be another rung further up the ladder! This wine is made from fifty-year-old vines and exudes prunes, liquorice, pepper, raspberries, spice and leather. It is viscous and saturated with purple, powerful fruit and seasoned with sweet oak nuances. I adore this over-the-top style. Serve it slightly chilled, give it a bit of air – half an hour in a decanter – and set it up with a huge, carnivorous dinner. It will take you weeks to get the grin off your face.

£14.50 **Gigondas, Château de Saint Cosme**, 1999, Southern Rhône, France (**Decorum, Handford, Harvey Nichols and Noel Young**). Seventy-year-old vines give up their noble harvest for this extraordinary wine. Gigondas is a neighbouring village to Châteauneuf-du-Pape and the

BLOCKBUSTER

wine styles are identical. The prices, thankfully, are not. Very few estates in the southern Rhône capture the awesome depth and texture that Louis Barroul manages for this insanely serious 'giggle-juice'. Do not think. Just flick to the directory, find the relevant merchant's numbers, and order. Quickly. There is no rush to drink this wine, but time is of the essence if you want to get hold of a few bottles.

£14.99 **Penfolds Cabernet Shiraz, Bin 389**, 1998, South Australia, Australia (**Boo, Bot, Maj, Odd, Sai, Saf and Tes**). Bin 28 (Kalimna Shiraz), Bin 128 (Coonawarra Shiraz) and Bin 407 (Cabernet Sauvignon) in 1998 are all superb wines. But the pick of the bunch is Bin 389, and it is also the most expensive, whoops. About half Shiraz, half Cab, this dense, almost black wine is stuffed with velvety smooth Ribena flavours, augmented by elements of espresso coffee, mint leaf, fresh spices and sweet wood smoke. It could live for fifteen years, but probably won't get the chance.

£14.99 **Villa Maria Reserve Merlot/Cabernet Sauvignon**, 1998, Hawkes Bay, New Zealand (**OFW, Saf and Wimbledon**). 1998 was a landmark vintage for reds in the Hawkes Bay area. The grapes for this wine come from an old, dried-up riverbed. The gravelly soils are perfect for keeping the vines feet (roots) warm at night and ensure a really ripe crop. This is the best Villa Maria red I have ever tasted. The palate starts off huge and rebounds over and over again with whooshes of blackcurrant fruit. It is a monster chocolatey, Ribena-soaked red.

£16.99 **Bannockburn Shiraz, Geelong**, 1999, Victoria, Australia (**Ballantynes, Bennetts, Carringtons, OFW, Philglas and Tanners**). This is one of my favourite Australian red wines. Although you may be fooled into saying it was French if you tasted it blind. This is because the oak, spice and wonderful, aromatic black fruit intensity is a dead ringer for mega-quality, top vintage Côte-Rôtie. Bannockburn should hit the shelves in December '01, so be patient if you bought this book in October! But, with decent Côte-Rôtie costing well over twenty quid and needing at least five years to smooth itself out, this wine looks like a veritable steal. Make an orderly queue.

£19.50 **Planeta Santa Cecilia**, 1999, Sicily, Italy (**La Réserve, Sai, Valvona & Crolla and Wimbledon**). Hedonistic stuff. Nothing comes close to this version of Nero d'Avola. Here it is at its peak of perfection. It is the vinous equivalent of an orchestra belting out Rachmaninoff's Piano Concerto No. 2 in C minor or, if you like, Radiohead playing live. So, with the volume knob at eleven, check out this supreme being. A tasting note would not do it justice, just think red wine and multiply by a zillion.

£19.99 **Ravenswood Lane Reunion Shiraz**, 1998, Adelaide Hills, South Australia, Australia (**Amps, D. Byrne, Jeroboam, Noble Rot, Sommelier and Noel Young**). Whenever I taste awesome Shiraz I always make a tasting note linking the complexity and power to that of Côte-Rôtie, the northern Rhône home of the Syrah (Shiraz) grape. This wine is no exception. It is a deluxe creature, made by man mountain John Edwards – a man with an appetite for life similar to that of a viking.

£19.99 **Wakefield St Andrews Shiraz**, 1998, Clare Valley, Australia (**Bacchanalia, Evertons, Laithwaites, Raeburn and Roberts & Speight**). Put your seat belt on. I tasted twenty Clare Valley Shirazs blind and picked this as the winner, on exuberance, flamboyance and notes like 'serious, superb, stunning, delish and love it'. But is that because most Clare Valley Shirazs are somewhat leaner and restrained? Maybe. Regardless, this wine is spectacular. Rather than take up another position in my Top 250 with 1998 Wakefield St Andrews Cabernet, at the same price, from the same merchants, I have squeezed it into this one. Oh, guess what? I marked this Cab as the best in a blind tasting of twenty-one from Clare Valley. So I reckon this is an estate to watch.

£20.99 **Spice Route Wine Company, Flagship Syrah**, 1999, Malmesbury, South Africa (**Wimbledon**). Huge, rich fruit and fabulous concentration are the foundations of this perfect wine. Eben Sadie, the surf dude winemaker, is a fan of Côte-Rôtie. That makes sense, as this Syrah is easily as impressive as many Côte-Rôties I have tasted. I wonder what the French would say about this monumental achievement? Incidentally, it's not just Syrah that blows my mind on this estate – Merlot and Cabernet do as well, so look out for them. But back to the Syrah, which although able to be opened now for academic reasons, should really be kept in a darkened room for a few (five to ten) years. The problem is that by next year it will have all sold out, so you have to get your skates on now. Go.

£25.99 **Peter Lehmann Eight Songs Shiraz**, 1997/8, Barossa Valley, South Australia, Australia (**OFW and Wai**). 1996 was the first vintage of Eight Songs. It is a great wine. Since then, the 1997 has hit the spotlight and it is truly magnificent. The 1998 is imminent and for me is even better than the preceding two vintages – maybe even a masterpiece. But whichever year you track down, you are in for a treat. Eight Songs is a monster of a Barossa Shiraz (a plum, chocolate, pepper-frenzy), tempered by a spell in top notch French oak barrels. I think that in a few years it will be regarded as one of the all-time great Aussie wines. At the moment, not enough people have had a go at it to spread the word. This is where you guys come in. Just don't all rush in immediately – we don't want the price to go up, do we?

BLOCKBUSTER

£4.49 half bottle, **Moscato d'Asti, Nivole, Chiarlo**,
2000, Piedmont, Italy (**Averys, Odd, Vino Vino and
Wimbledon**). This dinky little fizzy half bot of effervescent
grapey Muscat is one of the cutest wines around. If you
are having a fruity pudding, or just sitting in front of
the telly and need a boost, then this will recharge your
batteries. It is delightfully sweet in a 'ripe fruit' way not
a sugary one, so it does not cloy or hang around on the
palate. It is like a tiny capsule of summeriness, that you
can uncork whenever you need a hit.

£5.99 **Brown Brothers Late Harvested Muscat**,
2000, Victoria, Australia (**Boo, Maj, Mor, Odd and Tanners**).
This is the model to which all other sweet wines have to
aspire. The case for this wine is as follows: I have been
buying it for fourteen years, and year in, year out, it is spot
on. This full bottle sells for a mere £5.99 to £6.49 and is
loaded with melon, papaya, honey and peach, but is in no
way cloying or oily. Chilled down ice-cold, it is one of the
cleanest apéritifs around (n.b. be ahead of fashion and
serve light, clean sweeties to kick off a dinner party). It is
the definitive pudding wine for apple crumble and all things
fruit-tart-like. After a hard day this will perk you up like no
other wine. The case against… nothing, your honour.

£5.99 half bottle, **Brown Brothers Orange Muscat
& Flora**, 2000, Victoria, Australia (**Boo, Coo, Maj, Odd,
Peckham & Rye, Sai, Tanners, Thr, Wai and WRa**). Orange
Muscat is the definitive, fail-safe choccy wine and Brown

Brothers have been selling this wine in the UK for nearly twenty years. The nose is orange blossom scented and the palate is mandarin, honey, tangerine and brandy snap-soaked. This 2000 vintage is the best yet. Orange and chocolate is already a proven, working partnership – just ask Terry.

£5.99 half bottle, **Lenz Moser, Beerenauslese**, 1999, Austria (**Charles Hennings and Tes**). Apparently over three hundred Tesco stores stock this wine. What a result! You have no excuse to avoid one of the bargain elixirs of the known solar system. A stunner in every sense, 'beerenauslese' means 'individually selected very ripe grapes'. The grapes used here are ultra-ripe and make it an unctuous, tropical, perfectly balanced sweet wine. A half bot will easily do six glasses. Not bad for a pound a glass! Grab a bottle, because the weather conditions were not right in 2000 to make this wine, so there is a shortage looming.

£6.99 half bottle, **Bonterra Vineyards Muscat**, 1999, California, USA (**Odd, Sai and Wai**). This organic Muscat will ease you into the sweet wine thing, particularly if you are not usually a sticky fan. The Californian wine giant Fetzer make this heavenly brew, and they manage to capture Muscat's light, honeyed, grapey, clean notes perfectly. It will taste drier than it really is with a heavy pudding; however, you will be left in a frisky, refreshed mood. The best way to enjoy it would be with strawberries, dipped in chocolate sauce.

£6.99 **Clairette de Die Tradition, Jadisanne**, NV, Rhône, France (**Wai**). Made from the juicy Muscat grape, this is a glorious, off-dry, sparkling wine with only 7% alcohol. You could say that it is a mild-mannered grapey fizz, masquerading as an up-market soda pop. Whatever, this organic Clairette is an elegant wine that will impress fans of Asti or Moscato. Like these two wines, Jadisanne is made from the Muscat grape, but unlike the crude sparkling wine method used for the two Italian wines, this is made using the traditional (Champagne) method. All in all it is a wonderful pudding wine for fruit-based dishes.

£6.99 half bottle, **Dindarello Maculan**, 2000, Veneto, Italy (**Odd and Valvona & Crolla**). You only need a dribble of this wine to get your taste buds boogying. It is made from semi-dried Moscato grapes which are fermented in the New Year after the harvest. This concentrates the sugars and makes for a cool, honeyed, white-peach-scented wine with delicate floral flavours and a well-balanced, not sticky or sickly, finish. The acidity is fairly tangy and the fruitiness, not sweetness, of the Moscato shines through.

£6.99 50cl bottle, **Domaine Léonce Cuisset**, 1998, Saussignac, France (**Sai**). Light and creamy, with a wonderful almondy, fruity flavour, this beautiful honey and spring-blossom-scented wine will adore being twinned with fruity/pastry puddings. Made in the same way as Sauternes, it benefits price-wise from a lowlier postcode – Saussignac – but lacks nothing in style and elegance.

naughty and *boozy*

£7.99 50cl bottle, **Visanto, Boutari**, 1995, Santorini, Greece (**Odd**). This is one of the most impressive sweet wines of the year. The overpriced Vin Santos of Tuscany must watch out, because this wine is stealing their thunder, at a much lower price. Vino di Santorini is the wine that gave its name to the Vin Santos of Italy. The process of drying the grapes to concentrate their sugar, and then maturing the wickedly sweet wine in oak barrels, is well practised. But nowhere does it taste as naughty and boozy as this wine – a seriously sweet, caramel-coloured, awesomely heady, marmalade and honey infusion.

£8.99 half bottle, **Brown Brothers Noble Riesling**, 1998, Victoria, Australia (**Boo, Bot, Penistone and WRa**). This is an absolute stonker. It is made from botrytis-affected grapes (affected by 'noble rot' which concentrates the sugar in the grape giving a very sweet wine). The result? An intense, heady, liquidised fruit bowl of a wine that is toffeed and refreshingly citrusy at the same time. This balancing act between unctuous sweetness and a clean finish is amazing. You only need a teeny glass to feel the force, so pour carefully.

£8.99 **Moscato d'Asti, Bricco Quaglia, La Spinetta**, 2000, Piedmont, Italy (**La Réserve and Wimbledon**). Wow, spending a tenner on a sparkling Muscat, are you sure? Asti Martini is only a fiver and it is not bad, but Bricco Quaglia is five times the wine. In fact I think it is one of the best sweet/sparkling wines in the world. Classically aromatic, with rich, mouth-filling Moscato (Italian for Muscat) juice, this is the epitome of grapeyness, with a fairy-light, super-refreshing finish. It is rather like a jet of crushed grape juice from an ice-cool soda siphon.

£8.99 **Sigalas Mezzo**, 1999, Santorini, Greece (**Odd**). A handful of Greek wines have made it into my Top 250, and Sigalas led the way. Made from the Assyrtiko grape, this gorgeous wine is a slightly lighter Greek version of the Tuscan sweetie Vin Santo. The grapes are picked and then raisined a touch to concentrate the honeyed, oily grape juice. The result is an orange zest, sherbet, honey, almonds and dribbly spongecake-infused creation. It is also a bargain price for a 75cl bottle. Yum.

£9.79 half bottle, **Château Liot, Sauternes**, 1997, Bordeaux, France (**Wai**). This half bottle of scrumptious Sauternes is a relative steal in a land of astronomically priced wines. I tasted this château alongside a few more famous names and it definitely had the edge, at half the price. The honeyed palate coupled with the restrained aroma of tropical fruit and creamy, sweet pastry nuances make it a real winner.

£11.95 **Muscat de Beaumes-de-Venise, Domaine de Durban**, 1999, Southern Rhône, France (**Berry Bros.**). Durban is my favourite domaine producing this famous Muscat incarnation. It is also less expensive than most of the competition – this is the price for a 75cl bottle. Clean, elegant, cool, wonderfully grapey and seriously sexy, this wine is one of the most relaxed ways to finish a feast. Small glasses are usually the order of the day for pudding wines, but I predict they will be topped up at a furious pace, so in order to expend less energy acting as a wine waiter, use a big glass just this once.

£13.95 half bottle, **Mount Horrocks, Cordon Cut Riesling**, 2000, Clare Valley, Australia (**Bennetts, Ben Ellis, Grog Blossom, Harvey Nichols, Mills Whitcombe, Philglas, Portland Wine and Shaw's**). I recently tasted a flight of six vintages of this wine, and they age like clockwork. The 2000 is certainly one of the finest wines made at Mount Horrocks and it will undoubtedly manage to live for a further eight or so years, but I suspect that it will be polished off in a trice. My tasting notes are – brûlée, candied orange, rhubarb, racy acidity, not overly sweet, mouth-coatingly luxurious. It is not cheap, but it is worth every penny when you feel this exotically sensual liquid glide over your palate.

£14.95 half bottle, **De Bortoli Noble One, Botrytised Sémillon**, 1999, New South Wales, Australia (**Australian Wine Club, Averys, Berry Bros., John Harvey, Lea & Sandeman, O.W. Loeb, Nobody Inn, OFW and Reid**). After a light vintage in 1997, and a small harvest in 1998, it is great to see De Bortoli hit the jackpot again in 1999. Incidentally, some of the stockists mentioned may still be selling older vintages: don't worry, they are all brilliant! In fact, every year since 1982, except for 1989 (torrential downpours), has resulted in succulent, luxurious, hypnotic concoctions. Sadly the French version of this wine (top Sauternes like Château d'Yquem) is far too dear at this kind of quality and on many occasions, in wine-tasting competitions, this turbo-charged honey, caramel-drenched wine has beaten France at its own game. Noble One is worth every penny.

£14.99 50cl bottle, **Tokaji Aszú, 5 Puttonyos, Royal Tokaji Company**, 1996, Hungary (**Berry Bros., Maj and Tanners**). Pronounced 'Tock-eye', this wine is rich, nutty, dark, almost burnt and much less tropical than my other recommended Tokaji (see below). If anything, ease your way into the style via the next bottle and then go for it with this more intense, less forgiving, more authentic version. Food-wise, this bottle can tackle trickier dishes such as sticky toffee pudding, treacle tart and pecan pie. And remember, a 50cl bottle can serve eight glasses.

£18.99 50cl bottle, **Tokaji Aszú, 5 Puttonyos, Domaine Disznókó**, 1993, Hungary (**Odd**). Tokaji has a flavour that sits somewhere between majestic Sauternes and a nutty, tangy sherry. I realise that there is a lot of room between these two wines, but imagine a terrifically honeyed wine with a walnut and crème brûlée aroma, and a candied orange peel finish. If you have got your mind around that, you will just have to go out and buy some of this. It is expensive, but the flavour is explosive and well worth the money.

£19.99 half bottle, **Mission Hill Vidal Icewine**, 1999, Okanagan Valley, British Columbia, Canada (**Wai**). Talk about exclusive; this wine is only available at Waitrose on the King's Road in London. There is not much stock, but at twenty pounds a half bottle I doubt that it will fly out the door too quickly. Each year Mission Hill chooses the best frozen grapes to make their icewine. In 1999 it was the turn of Vidal, a grape not dissimilar to Riesling. As the EU only managed to allow icewine into Europe this year, this sticky is somewhat of a landmark. What does it taste like? The sweetest tropical fruit elixir you could possibly imagine.

£21.99 **Billecart-Salmon, Demi-Sec**, NV, Champagne, France (**Bentalls, Fortnum & Mason, Odd and Uncorked**). The last of the Billecart foursome is officially a pudding wine, but it could never be described as sweet. Demi-Sec – half dry – is a weird classification, as this wine is really a richer, rounder version of the non-vintage wine. If you tasted it on its own it would certainly feel broad, ripe and a touch sweet, but with light puddings a bone-dry wine would taste too austere – so this cuvée comes into its own. Stick to fruity puds, and avoid syrupy ones, otherwise you will lose the elegance of this wine. It is perfect for weddings – as the toasts are often done during pudding!

£4.99 half bottle, **Magill Tawny, Penfolds**, NV, Barossa Valley, South Australia, Australia (**Bot, Maj, Saf, Thr, Unw and WRa**). A curious number. A tawny-port-style Australian wine made from two classic Aussie red grapes – Grenache and Shiraz. After fermentation and fortification, the wine is matured in a sherry-like fashion. Got it? The result is, of course, spectacular, with raisin, mocha-scent, burnt toffee and leather all hovering above the sweet Christmas puddingy palate. A glass of this will put hairs on your chest.

£5.59 **Waitrose Solera Jerezana Dry Amontillado**, NV, Jerez, Spain (**Wai**). A bone-dry sherry, like manzanilla, is a super, if unfashionable apéritif. But if you find yourself confronted by a nutty, rich, caramel-scented amontillado then grab some grub. The rich, raisiny fruit and stupendous, dry finish are amazing, particularly with robust, hearty soups (see Food and Wine Section). If you have not tried this combination before then please give it a go. It is one of the most illuminating and unlikely matches of all.

£5.59 **Waitrose Solera Jerezana Rich Cream Sherry**, NV, Jerez, Spain (**Wai**). I am a huge fan of cream sherry when tackling a tricky coffee, toffee or nut-flavoured pudding. Chilled down, the gloriously rich flavour is nutty and luxuriously sweet. And, as this is a full bottle (as opposed to a half), it will last for ages, is great value and you'll have something to serve your vicar if he pops in. Don't worry about any anti-sherry-snobs; they are the ones who are missing out on this heavenly combination.

£6.49 half bottle, **Campbells Rutherglen Muscat**, NV, Victoria, Australia (**Odd, Philglas, Christopher Piper, Reid and Noel Young**). This little beautifully packaged creation is a true sipping-style pudding wine. Campbells coats the mouth wonderfully, hanging around on the palate for minutes. You do not need a full bottle of this wine, as it can stretch to six glasses and is amazingly satisfying. The raisin, rose petal and vanilla fudge aromas will haunt you for hours, and the exquisitely balanced palate seems to start off with a fruity, toffeed flavour then recede gracefully to a crème brûlée-taste tingle.

£7.95 half bottle, **Vintage Mas Amiel, Maury**, 1997, Roussillon, France (**Lea & Sandeman**). Maury is a tiny area in the southwest corner of France producing a port-like wine from the Grenache grape. The beauty of this wine is that it does not have the high alcohol level of port and it is ready to drink very young. Mas Amiel is stunning, and will reward the drinker who either sips it after dinner with bitter, dark chocolate, or, in true Gallic style, as a tiny, refreshing, cool apéritif before a meal.

£7.99 **Warre's Warrior Special Reserve**, NV, Douro, Portugal (**Asd, Bot, Coo, Mor, Odd, Saf, Sai, Som, Tes, Thr, Unw, Wai, WCe and WRa**). You simply have to have a bottle of port at Christmas and with so many to choose from, why not plump for a winner? The multi-award winning Symington family makes this super wine. Warrior just happens to be one of the best value ports on the

shelves and gives you everything you'd expect from this
noble style of wine. It's what I'll be drinking this Christmas.
Intense plummy fruit, a kick of spice and a rich, long warming
finish are all here in abundance. I hope you buy a few bottles
for the crowd in December.

£7.99   half bottle, **Yalumba Museum Release Muscat**,
NV, South Australia, Australia (**Bennetts and La Réserve**).
You will get eight glasses from this luxurious half bottle, as
every micro-sip of Yalumba's nectar permeates your entire
olfactory system. Museum Release is ten years old and
made from the Muscat variety. It is not dissimilar to
liquidised trifle, gingerbread and coffee cake combined,
all finished off with a liberal spoonful of treacle. Mouth-
coating and light years long on the palate, this wine would
satisfy even the sweetest tooth in the country. Drink with
intense puds or sip while lying down. Or keep it in a hip-
flask for touchline resuscitation on a cold winter's day.

£8.19   **Tio Pepe, Extra Dry Fino Sherry, González
Byass**, NV, Jerez, Spain (**Asd, Bot, Coo, Mor, Odd, Saf,
Sai, Tes, Thr, Unw, Wai, WCe and WRa**). González Byass
is the most famous name in sherry. They have, at last,
redesigned their old, dowdy, brown-bottled Tio Pepe, which
now sports a fetching, chic, green glass livery. The wine
inside is still as good as ever, with its bone-dry, cleansing,
tangy, yeasty, grown-up flavour. So now you don't have
to feel old-fashioned if you enjoy dry sherry. You can drink
the best-selling Fino around and look cool at the same time.

drop-dead gorgeous

£8.95 **Pedro Ximénez, Solera Superior, Valdespino**,
NV, Jerez, Spain (**Lea & Sandeman**). A ridiculously luxurious
mouthful of drunken raisins, espresso coffee and burnt
toffee. Hard to believe that this fellow is a sherry. Shock
horror, but 'PX', as it is known, is every ice cream dish's
secret weapon. Very few wines actually complement ice
cream, and not only can you drink a glass of PX alongside
coffee, chocolate or vanilla-based ices, you could even
drizzle it on top. But please don't tell anyone I told you
to do this!

£9.99 **Taylors LBV**, 1996, Douro, Portugal (**Asd, Bot, Maj,
Mor, Odd, Saf, Sai, Som, Tes, Thr, Wai and WRa**). This
excellent 1996 Late Bottled Vintage follows fast on the
heels of the superbly repackaged 1995, and it doesn't take
its foot off the gas. You will not be disappointed when you
discover the awesome presence and brooding power of this
black-ink-stained port. Plum, blackberry, smoky oak and
enormous, mouth-filling weight ensure that this is a 'sitting
down' glass of wine. The palate finishes as smoothly as an
Aston Martin, and the aftertaste is staggeringly long.

£9.99 50cl bottle, **Warre's Otima, 10-year-old Tawny**,
NV, Douro, Portugal (**Asd, Bot, Coo, Odd, Saf, Sai, Tes, Thr,
Wai and WRa**). Apart from being one of the most eye-
catching bottles in the wine world, this tawny port is also
drop-dead gorgeous in the taste department. The bright
amber/ mahogany hue is coupled with a fragrance of
Callard and Bowser toffees and sweet plums. This is followed

by a nutty, raisin cake and sweet berry palate that tails off (eventually) into a yeasty, dry, savoury finish. Chill it a touch, pour and mellow out.

£10.95 **Banyuls, Tradition, Domaine de la Casa Blanca**, 1998, Roussillon, France (**La Vigneronne**). Another unmissable bottle from one of the UK's most exciting wine merchants. La Vig is like an Aladdin's Cave for wine lovers. Their Banyuls, made from the hardy grape Grenache, is a cross between a tawny port and a fine red wine. Served chilled, in little glasses, port lovers will marvel at this wine's elegance and poise. If you find port too fiery and alcoholic then try this as it is lighter, milder and smoother, with less of a spiry feel. The flavours within are chocolate, vanilla, cherry, raisin and coffee. An epic pudding or after-dinner wine – sheer perfection.

£11.99 **Blandy's 1994 Harvest Malmsey**, 1994, Madeira (**Direct Wines, Patrick Grubb, Maj and Wine Society**). This jolly Malmsey is made from the exceptional 1994 vintage and is enjoyable at a much younger age than normal Madeira. You may feel the need to drink some wine with your Christmas pudding and perhaps bank on having some spare for chocolate, treacle pudding, fruitcake etc. If so, this is the wine. Unfashionable but oh so impressive, and it lasts forever in the bottle. The rich amber, golden colour is followed with a raisin, coffee, toffee, chocolate and honey palate. You can't get more festive than this.

GAZETTEER

GRAPE VARIETIES

Before we head off around the world on my tour of great estates, I have listed names and short descriptions of some of the most important red and white grape varieties. These should give you an idea of the flavours of the wines mentioned in this chapter and my Top 250.

REDS

Cabernet Franc
Cabernet Franc lends a certain aromatic quality to a red wine, with good acidity, *black fruit* flavours and a *green, leafy* smell.

Cabernet Sauvignon
Long-lived Cabernet Sauvignon is the backbone of many huge red wines. Its hallmarks are a deep colour, *blackcurrant* flavour, with a *cigar-box* or *cedarwood* note and sometimes even a *dark-chocolate* texture and flavour.

Gamay
Gamay is a totally underrated, early-drinking grape producing wines which range in taste from summer *strawberry juice* and *red berry* lightness to wintry, robust, *black cherry* and *pepper* concoctions.

Grenache
Grenache, usually blended – often with Syrah (or Shiraz, 'down under') – is a *meaty, earthy, black-fruit*-drenched variety sometimes picking up a *herbal* scent not dissimilar to aromatic *pipe smoke*.

Malbec
This heavyweight grape offers deep colour, *black fruit* flavours and is often enriched with a dollop of *oak*.

Merlot

A juicy grape, with supple, smooth, velvety, *blackberry*, *plum*, *red wine gums* and *fruitcake* flavours. It is often accompanied by a touch of *oak*.

Mourvèdre

This rich, *plum* and *damson*-flavoured variety is often made into powerful, earthy wine.

Nebbiolo

An immensely tough grape that often needs five years in bottle to be even approachable in the glass. A great Nebbiolo can conjure up intense *plummy* flavours with *leathery*, *spicy*, *gamey* overtones.

Pinotage

Pinotage is an *earthy*, *spicy*, deeply coloured grape with *tobacco* and *plums* on the nose, crushed *berry fruit* on the palate and a hearty finish.

Pinot Noir

When on form, the Pinot Noir nose is often reminiscent of *wild strawberries*, *violets* and *redcurrants*, with a *black cherry* flavour on the palate. There is usually a degree of *oakiness* apparent, depending on the style. As these wines age, they take on a slightly *farmyardy* character and as the colour fades from dark to pale brick red, the nose can turn *leathery* and *raspberry*-like.

Sangiovese

This grape has *red fruit* flavours (*cherry* and *cranberry)* on the nose with a whiff of *fresh-cut herbs* and *leather* and an acidic kick on the finish.

Syrah/Shiraz

Syrah invokes explosive *blackberry* and *ground pepper* aromas with *vanilla*, *smoke* and *toasty oak* nuances. In the New World, big, inky-black Shiraz (the Syrah synonym) has high alcohol and a mouth-filling *prune* and *spice* palate.

Tempranillo

Ranging in flavour from *sweet vanilla* and *strawberry* to dark, brooding and *black cherry*, Tempranillo is the main variety in Rioja and many other Spanish red wines.

Zinfandel

'Zin' tastes like a turbo-charged *blackberry* meets a *spice* warehouse.

WHITES

Albariño/Alvarinho

A particularly good example can have a *peachy* aroma like Viognier, and a *flowery*, *spicy* palate like Riesling.

Aligoté

Aligoté produces a dry, lean apéritif style of wine that is designed to drink young.

Chardonnay

From neutral and characterless to wildly exotic, you can find *honey*, *butter*, *freshly baked bread*, *nuts*, *vanilla*, *butterscotch*, *orange blossom* and fresh *meadow flowers* in a top Chardonnay.

Chenin Blanc

This makes zippy, dry apéritif wines, medium-dry, food-friendly wines and full-on *honey* and succulent *peach* sweeties dripping in unctuous, mouth-filling richness.

Gewürztraminer

Gewürztraminer has the most distinctive smell of any single grape variety. Pungent *lychee*, *spice* and *rose petal* on the nose are accompanied, more often than not, by *oiliness* on the palate and a long, ripe finish. This grape has the unusual knack of always smelling sweet, and then surprising you by tasting bone dry.

Manseng
Gros and Petit Manseng both have a complex nose and *citrusy*, *floral* palate accompanied by a crisp finish. They are also found in sweet form.

Marsanne
Plump, rich and oily, Marsanne makes hefty foody wines.

Muscat
Muscat wines vary from the lightest, fizzy soda-siphon grape juice, like fairy dust dancing on your tongue, to the deepest, darkest, headiest liqueur like a rugby player's liniment. The common factor in all of these wines is that Muscat is the only grape variety that actually tastes of *grapes*.

Pinot Blanc/Pinot Bianco
Almost all the Pinot Blanc made worldwide is unoaked, dry and relatively inexpensive, tasting vaguely *appley*, *creamy* and *nutty*.

Riesling
Riesling produces a vast array of wine styles, from bone-dry apéritifs, through structured and foody, via long-lived, complex and off-dry, ending up at heart-achingly-beautiful sweeties. *Rhubarb*, *petrol*, *honey*, *honeysuckle* and *spice* are there in varying degrees.

Roussanne
Generally lean and aromatic, with hints of *apricot* and h*oney*. When on top form, Roussanne takes well to oak barrels and can provide a welcome change of direction for Chardonnay drinkers.

Sauvignon Blanc
An up-front, brazen, outgoing, happy-go-lucky style, with pristine, e*lderflower*-scented, refreshing, zesty, *citrusy* fruit.

Sémillon
The dominant aromas in dry Sémillon are *honey* and *lime juice*, and in sweet form are *honey*, and more *honey*.

Tokay-Pinot Gris/Pinot Grigio
The flavour of Tokay-Pinot Gris is somewhere between Pinot Blanc and Gewürztraminer. The distinctive nose of this grape is one of *spice*, *fruit* and *honey*. It does not have the *rose-petal*-perfumed element of Gewürz, and tends to be drier, like Pinot Blanc. Italy's Pinot Grigio is more akin to Aligoté.

Viognier
In the best examples Viognier offers a haunting perfume of *peach kernels* and *apricot blossom,* followed by an ample body with plenty of charm and a lingering aftertaste.

WINE REGIONS OF THE WORLD

In this chapter we look at the major wine regions in the world, and my favourite wineries within each. I have avoided wineries that churn out passable, average wines and any who have chanced on one-hit-wonder wines. Instead, I have focussed on the benchmark, top quality, talent-driven, rewarding wineries which have set my palate buzzing. You can rely on these guys when you are shopping for home drinking, in a restaurant, on holiday or when buying a present for a friend. Occasionally you'll find a producer or winery whose name is in **bold**. These I deem to be outstanding, where every wine made is mind-blowing. If a producer is both in **bold** and has a **£**, it means that its wines are expensive (£25 plus). These platinum-plated names are the money-no-object, whack-'em-on-your-Christmas-list wines, for those with a no-upper-limit mentality. That doesn't mean that every wine they make is unaffordable, far from it. Their main, flagship wine may be crazily dear, but their other labels may be brilliant and significantly cheaper. So, do not dismiss these wineries, as they always pop up in bin-end sales, auctions or on independent merchants' wine lists. Those **bold** estates without a **£** make some eminently more affordable wines (some in their range retail from £5 to £25), so keep an eye out for them. These may just be the wineries for you.

A short list of the best recent vintages is included after some regions.

AUSTRALIA

Battling hard for world wine supremacy, Australia continues to forge ahead since its explosion onto the market in the mid-eighties. From then on, the entire industry down under has worked together to promote Australian wines with gusto. It is fair to say that an average bottle of Aussie wine is the safest on the shelves. Any country would be delighted if their supposed lowest common denominators were as good as Jacob's Creek and Banrock Station. Wine lovers are embracing these fruit-driven styles and have been encouraged to trade up to such a degree that Australia has overtaken France on the UK market. Well done Australia, you have shocked the Old World into pulling its socks up. I probably drink as much Aussie wine as French these days, largely because there is every style of wine under the sun to choose from – with outstanding examples made by the winemakers below.

WESTERN AUSTRALIA

The top producers are – Alkoomi, Amberley, **Brookland Valley**,

Cape Mentelle, **Cullens**, Devil's Lair, Evans & Tate, Frankland Estate, Howard Park, **Leeuwin Estate**, **Moss Wood**, Plantagenet, Picardy, Pierro, Vasse Felix, Voyager, Wignalls and Xanadu.

SOUTH AUSTRALIA
The top producers are – **Tim Adams**, d'Arenberg, **Ashton Hills**, Balnaves, **Barratt**, Jim Barry, Bowen, Grant Burge, Chain of Ponds, Charles Cimicky, Coriole, Crabtree, **Henschke**, Elderton, **Grosset**, Hardy's, Heritage, Hillstowe, Steve Hoff, **Hollick**, **Katnook**, Leasingham, **Peter Lehmann**, **Lenswood**, Lindemans, Maglieri, Majella, Charlie Melton, Mitchell, Mountadam, **Mount Horrocks**, **Nepenthe**, Parker, **Penfolds**, Penley, Petaluma, Pewsey Vale, Pikes, Primo Estate, **Ravenswood Lane**, Rockford, **Rosemount**, **Shaw & Smith**, Skillogalee, **St Hallett**, **Torbreck**, Turkey Flat, Wakefield (Taylors), **Geoff Weaver**, Wendouree, Wynns and **Yalumba**.

Top South Australian red vintages – I like these wines young. Ten years old is probably the peak, save for only one or two labels: 1986, 1990, 1991, 1994, 1996, 1997, 1998, 1999 and 2000.

NEW SOUTH WALES
The top producers are – Allandale, **Brokenwood**, **Simon Gilbert**, Lindemans, Logan Wines, Mount Pleasant, **Rosemount**, Rothbury and Tyrrell's.

VICTORIA
The top producers are – Baileys, Bannockburn, **Bleasdale**, Brown Brothers, **Campbells**, Chandon, **Coldstream Hills**, Crawford River, **Dalwhinnie**, **De Bortoli**, **Diamond Valley Vineyards**, **Giaconda £**,

Jasper Hill, Michelton, Mount Langi Ghiran, Métier Wines, **Mount Mary,** Phillip Island Vineyard, Redbank, Scotchman's Hill, Taltarni, T'Gallant, David Traeger, Virgin Hills, Wild Duck Creek, Yeringberg, Yarra Burn and **Yarra Yering £.**

TASMANIA
The top producers – Jansz and **Pipers Brook.**

AUSTRIA
A short, but essential list of producers making epic dry whites and sweeties – **Weingut Bründlmayer,** Schloß Gobelsburg, **Franz Hirtzberger, Alois Kracher** and Willi Opitz.

CANADA
A relative newcomer to our market, but Canada is set for a huge following, thanks to some great whites and wonderful sweet Icewines. **Best estates Burrowing Owl,** Château des Charmes, Henry of Pelham, **Inniskillin, Mission Hill,** Quail's Gate, Southbrook Farms and Sumac Ridge.

CHILE AND ARGENTINA
It seems that after the enormous rush on to the market some years ago, both Chile and Argentina have sat back and become a touch lazy. There are still some fantastic wines out there, but only if you stick to the best estates. Both countries need to concentrate more, now that South Africa, Australia and New Zealand have knuckled down, for round two of the New World tussle.
Best Chilean estates Caliterra, Casa Lapostolle, Concha y Toro, Viña Cousiño Macul, **Errázuriz, MontGras, Miguel Torres,** San Pedro,

Valdivieso and **Veramonte**.
Best Argentinian estates La Agricola (the 'Q' range), **Nicolas Catena**, **Finca El Retiro**, **Norton**, **Santa Julia**, Valentin Bianchi and Bodegas Weinert.

FRANCE
BORDEAUX
The majority of worthwhile Bordeaux reds fall into **bold** territory, and as prices are generally fearfully expensive, these wines are usually reserved for special occasions. When putting this list together I was very hard on the region and have culled a large, rambling list down to a hard core of superb châteaux. This is where the masterful red grapes Cabernet Sauvignon, Merlot and Cabernet Franc hold court. The percentages of each in the final wine vary from château to château but you can be sure that whatever the final blend, the wine will have spent some time slumbering in oak barrels. This recipe is pretty much the benchmark for red wine around the globe. Go for it, if you are feeling flush.

RED WINES
THE LEFT BANK
Margaux d'Angludet, Cantemerle, **Durfort-Vivens**, d'Issan, La Lagune, Lascombes, **Margaux £**, **Palmer £** and Rausan-Ségla.
Moulis and Listrac Chasse-Spleen and Poujeaux.
St-Julien Clos du Marquis, **Ducru-Beaucaillou £**, Gruaud-Larose, Lagrange, **Léoville-Barton £**, **Léoville-Las-Cases £**, **Léoville-Poyferré £**, St-Pierre and Talbot.
Pauillac Batailley, **Grand-Puy-Lacoste £**, Haut-Bages-Libéral, Haut-Batailley, **Lafite-Rothschild £**, **Latour £**, Les Forts de Latour,

Lynch-Bages **£**, **Mouton-Rothschild £**, **Pichon-Longueville Baron £**, **Pichon-Longueville-Comtesse de Lalande £** and Pontet-Canet.

St-Estèphe Beau-Site, Le Boscq, Calon-Ségur, **Cos d'Estournel £**, Haut-Marbuzet, Lafon-Rochet, **Montrose £**, Les-Ormes-de-Pez and Phélan-Ségur.

Haut-Médoc and (Bas) Médoc Arnauld, Citran, Lanessan, Les Ormes-Sorbet, Malescasse, Patache d'Aux, Potensac, **Sociando-Mallet**, La Tour de By, Tour du Haut-Moulin and Villegeorge.

Graves Bahans-Haut-Brion, **Les Carmes-Haut-Brion**, Chantegrive, Domaine de Chevalier, de Fieuzal, Haut-Bailly, **Haut-Brion £**, La Louvière, **La Mission-Haut-Brion £**, Pape-Clément, Picque-Caillou and Smith-Haut-Lafitte.

THE RIGHT BANK

St-Emilion Angélus **£**, L'Arrosée, **Ausone £**, Canon-La-Gaffelière, Chauvin, **Cheval Blanc £**, Clos Fourtet, Dassault, **La Dominique £**, Figeac, Larmande, Monbousquet, Le Tertre-Rôteboeuf, La Tour-du-Pin-Figeac and Troplong-Mondot.

Pomerol Beauregard, Bon Pasteur, Certan-Giraud, Certan-de-May, **Clinet £**, Clos du Clocher, Clos René, **La Conseillante £**, La Croix-St Georges, Domaine de l'Eglise, l'Eglise-Clinet, l'Enclos, **l'Evangile £**, La Fleur de Gay, Le Gay, Gazin, Lafleur, La Fleur-Pétrus, Latour à Pomerol, **Pétrus £**, Le Pin, **Trotanoy £** and **Vieux-Château-Certan £**.

Lalande-de-Pomerol Bel-Air, Belles-Graves and **La Fleur de Boüard**.

Canon-Fronsac and Fronsac Canon-Moueix, Fontenil, Hervé-Laroque, Mazeris, Moulin-Haut-Laroque, Rouet and **La Vieille-Cure**.

Côtes de Bourg and Blaye Haut-Sociando, **Roc des Cambes** and Tayac.

Top red Bordeaux vintages – The finest wines from the best châteaux can live happily for thirty or forty years; beyond that cross your fingers: 1945, 1947, 1949, 1955, 1959, 1961, 1962, 1966, 1970, 1982, 1983, 1985, 1986, 1988, 1989, 1990, 1995, 1996, 1998, 1999 and 2000.

DRY WHITE WINES
Graves Carbonnieux, **Domaine de Chevalier £**, de Fieuzal, **Haut-Brion £**, La Louvière, La Tour Martillac, **Laville-Haut-Brion £** and Smith-Haut-Lafitte.

SWEET WHITE WINES
Sauternes and **Barsac** d'Arche, Bastor-Lamontagne, Broustet, **Climens £**, Coutet, Doisy-Daëne, Doisy-Dubroca, Doisy-Védrines, de Fargues, Filhot, **Gilette £**, Guiraud, Les Justices, **Lafaurie-Peyraguey £**, Liot, de Malle, Nairac, **Rabaud-Promis £**, **Raymond-Lafon £**, Rayne-Vigneau, **Rieussec £**, **Suduiraut £**, **La Tour Blanche £** and **d'Yquem £**.

Top Sauternes vintages – The high sugar levels in this style of wine mean they can last for ages: 1945, 1949, 1955, 1959, 1967, 1971, 1975, 1976, 1983, 1986, 1988, 1989, 1990, 1996, 1997, 1998 and 1999.

BURGUNDY
The world-renowned white wonder, Chardonnay, and its equally starry red companion, Pinot Noir, have the leading roles in Burgundy. The zingy white grape Aligoté and much-derided red variety Gamay (Beaujolais) ably support them. This region is close to my heart and it has taken me a long time to unravel its

complexities. I am nowhere near to sussing it out completely, but it is certainly an enjoyable challenge. This list of domaines will, I hope, get you closer to the 'knowledge' that should help you to unlock the code to the most enigmatic region of all.

CHABLIS (white) Billaud-Simon, A. & F. Boudin, Daniel Dampt, **René & Vincent Dauvissat**, **Jean-Paul Droin**, Jean Durup, Louis Michel, Laurent Tribut and **François & Jean-Marie Raveneau.**

ST-BRIS-LE-VINEUX and CHITRY (white) Jean-Hugues Goisot and Christian Morin.

CÔTES DE NUITS
Marsannay-la-Côte and Fixin (mainly red) Charles Audoin, René Bouvier and Bruno Clair.
Gevrey-Chambertin (red) Claude Dugat, **Géantet-Pansiot**, Denis Mortet, Joseph Roty, **Armand Rousseau** and Serafin.
Morey-St-Denis (red) des Beaumont, **Domaine des Lambrays**, Dujac, Hubert Lignier and **Ponsot**.
Chambolle-Musigny (red) **Ghislaine Barthod**, Pierre Bertheau, Christian Clerget, Comte de Vogüé and **Georges & Christophe Roumier**.
Vosne-Romanée and **Flagey-Echézeaux** (red) Robert Arnoux, **de la Romanée-Conti £**, René Engel, **Jean Grivot**, Anne-Françoise Gros, **Leroy £**, **Méo-Camuzet**, Mongeard-Mugneret and Emanuel Rouget.
Nuits-St-Georges (red) Bertrand Ambroise, Jean Chauvenet, **Robert Chevillon**, Jean-Jacques Confuron, **Daniel Chopin-Groffier**, **Dominique Laurent**, Lécheneaut, Alain Michelot and Daniel Rion.

CÔTES DE BEAUNE

Aloxe-Corton & Ladoix-Serrigny (mainly red) Michel Voarick.

Pernand-Vergelesses (red and white) **Bonneau du Martray £**, Marius Delarche and Maurice Rollin.

Savigny-lès-Beaune (red and white) Maurice Ecard and **Jean-Marc Pavelot**.

Chorey-lès-Beaune (red) **Tollot-Beaut**.

Beaune (mainly red) Joseph Drouhin and Louis Jadot.

Pommard (red) Comte Armand, **Jean-Marc Boillot**, Madame de Courcel and **Hubert de Montille**.

Volnay (red) **Marquis d'Angerville**, **Michel Lafarge** and Roblet-Monnot.

Monthélie (red and white) Boussey.

Auxey-Duresses (red and white) Jean-Pierre Diconne and Claude Maréchal.

St-Romain (mainly white) Christophe Buisson and d'Auvenay.

Meursault (white) Michel Bouzereau, **Jean-François Coche-Dury £**, Vincent Dancer, Jean-Philippe Fichet, Patrick Javillier, **des Comtes Lafon £**, Marc Rougeot, **Guy Roulot** and Michel Tessier.

Puligny-Montrachet (white) Louis Carillon, Chartron & Trébuchet, **Leflaive** and **Etienne Sauzet**.

Chassagne-Montrachet (white) Guy Amiot, Blain-Gagnard, Colin-Deléger, Duperrier-Adam, Jean-Noël Gagnard, Gagnard-Delagrange, **Bernard Morey**, **Michel Niellon** and **Ramonet £**.

St-Aubin (red and white) Henri Prudhon and Gérard Thomas.

Santenay (red and white) Vincent Dureuil-Janthial and **Vincent Girardin**.

CÔTES CHALONNAISE
Rully (red and white) Eric de Suremain.
Mercurey (red and white) **Michel Juillot** and Antonin Rodet.
Givry (red and white) Joblot and François Lumpp.

MÂCONNAIS
(**Mâcon, Pouilly-Fuissé, St-Véran, Viré-Clessé**) (mainly white) Daniel Barraud, **André Bonhomme**, Cordier, Deux Roches, **Michel Forest**, **Château Fuissé** (Domaine Vincent), Goyard, Guillemot-Michel, Robert-Denogent, Talmard, **Jean Thevenet** and Verget (Guffens-Heynen is the domaine name).

BEAUJOLAIS
Producing mainly red wines the most highly regarded sub-regions are the ten Cru Villages: St-Amour, Juliénas, Fleurie, Moulin-à-Vent, Brouilly, Côte de Brouilly, Régnié, Chénas, Chiroubles and Morgon. The top producers are – Aucoeur, Champagnon, **Michel Chignard**, Coudert, Georges Duboeuf (domaine-bottled wines only), Henry Fessy, Maurice Gaget, **Pascal Granger**, Louis Jadot (**Château des Jacques**), **Paul Janin**, Bernard Mélinand, **Alain Passot**, **Jean-Charles Pivot** and Vissoux.

Top Burgundy vintages – Pinot Noir and Chardonnay drink well up to fifteen years old, thereafter get a little bit funky: 1969, 1971, 1978, 1980, 1985, 1988, 1989, 1990, 1995, 1996, 1997, 1998, 1999 and 2000.

CHAMPAGNE
This is a strange one. In my top 250, I have tracked down a few small Champagne houses that have made astonishing wines this

year, but they don't feature in this list of more famous names, and vice versa. The reason I have not included them here is because I need to see a constant pedigree of year on year releases before they make this elite list. The reason not all of the wines below appear in my Top 250 is that I would run out of space very quickly!

Billecart-Salmon *NV* Brut Réserve, Demi-Sec and Brut Rosé. *Vintage* Cuvée Nicolas-François Billecart, Elisabeth Salmon Rosé, Grande Cuvée and Blanc de Blancs.

Bollinger *NV* Special Cuvée. *Vintage* Grande Année, RD and Vieilles Vignes Françaises Blanc de Noirs.

Deutz *Vintage* Blanc de Blancs and Cuvée William Deutz.

Gosset *NV* Brut Excellence and Grande Réserve Brut. *Vintage* Grande Millésime Brut.

Charles Heidsieck *Vintage* Brut Millésime.

Jacquesson *Vintage* Blanc de Blancs, Dégorgement Tardive and Signature.

Krug £ *NV* Grande Cuvée. *Vintage* Vintage and Clos du Mesnil.

Laurent-Perrier *NV* Cuvée Rosé Brut. *Vintage* Grand Siècle 'La Cuvée'.

Moët & Chandon *Vintage* Cuvée Dom Pérignon Brut.

Pol Roger *NV* Brut 'White Foil'. *Vintage* Brut Vintage, Brut Chardonnay, Brut Rosé and Cuvée Sir Winston Churchill.

Louis Roederer *NV* Brut Premier. *Vintage* Blanc de Blancs, Brut Millésime and Cristal, Cristal Rosé.

Ruinart *Vintage* 'R' de Ruinart Brut and Dom Ruinart Blanc de Blancs.

Salon £ *Vintage* Blanc de Blancs.

Taittinger *NV* Brut Réserve. *Vintage* Comtes de Champagne Blanc de Blancs.

Veuve Clicquot *NV* Brut 'Yellow Label' and Demi-Sec. *Vintage* Vintage Réserve, La Grande Dame Brut and La Grande Dame Rosé.

Top Champagne vintages – Surprisingly long-lived if kept in good conditions: 1964, 1966, 1971, 1975, 1976, 1979, 1982, 1983, 1985, 1988, 1989, 1990, 1995, 1996, 1997, 1998, 1999 and 2000.

ALSACE

This under-priced, over-performing region provides us with some of the best foody, apéritif, decadently sweet and casual-drinking wines in the world. Grape varieties to seek out are Gewürztraminer, Riesling, Tokay-Pinot Gris, Muscat, Pinot Blanc and Sylvaner. Just avoid the reds and fizzies. The best producers are – Bott-Geyl, Boxler, Marcel Deiss, Hauller, Hugel, Kreydenweiss, Mann, Mittnacht-Klack, **Ostertag**, Rolly Gassmann, Schlumberger, Schoffit, André Thomas, **Trimbach**, **Weinbach** and **Zind-Humbrecht**.

Top Alsace vintages – Only Vendange Tardive and Sélection des Grains Nobles styles live for more than fifteen years: 1971, 1976, 1983, 1985, 1988, 1989, 1990, 1992, 1995, 1996, 1997, 1998, 1999 and 2000.

LOIRE VALLEY

My list follows the river Loire inland from the Atlantic, picking out only the greatest estates in this elongated, inexpensive region. Sauvignon Blanc and Chenin Blanc are the main white grapes grown here, with Chenin Blanc having full responsibility for making the sweeties, although it also makes dry and medium-sweet wines. The majority of the reds are made from Cabernet Franc, with Gamay and Pinot Noir stepping in for lighter styles.
Muscadet (white) Château de Chasseloir, **Vincent & Sébastian Chéreau** and Domaine de la Mortaine.

Savennières (white) Domaine des Baumards, Clos de la Coulée de Serrant and La Roche-aux-Moines.

Coteaux du Layon, Coteaux de l'Aubance, Bonnezeaux, Quarts de Chaume (white sweeties) Domaine des Baumards, **Château Pierre Bise**, Château de Fesles, **Vincent Lecointre**, de Petit Val, Didier Richou and de la Roulierie.

Sparkling Saumur Bouvet-Ladubay.

Saumur and **Saumur Champigny** (red and white) du Hureau, **Domaine Filliatreau**, Langlois-Château and Nerleux.

Chinon (mainly red) **Bernard Baudry**, Couly-Dutheil and Charles Joguet.

Saint-Nicolas de Bourgueil (red) Lamé-Delille-Boucard, Jean-Paul Mabileau and Max & Lydie Cognard-Taluau.

Bourgueil (red) **Pierre-Jacques Druet**, de l'Espy, Lamé-Delille-Boucard and Joël Taluau.

Vouvray (white) Bourillon-Dorléans, **Gaston Hue**t and Philippe Foreau.

Sauvignon de Touraine (white) **Alain Marcadet**.

Gamay de Touraine (red) **Henry Marionnet**.

Jasnières (white) **Joël Gigou** and Jean-Baptiste Pinon.

Cheverny (white) Salvard.

Sancerre (white, rosé and red) Sylvain Bailly, Bailly-Reverdy, Philippe de Benoist, **Henri Bourgeois**, **Cotat**, Daulny, Vincent Delaporte, André Dézat, Henri Natter, **Pascal & Nicolas Reverdy**, Vacheron and **André Vatan**.

Pouilly-Fumé (white) **Didier Dagueneau**, Serge Dagueneau, Jean-Claude Chatelain, Château du Nozet (de Ladoucette), **Michel Redde**, Hervé Seguin and **Château de Tracy**.

Menetou-Salon (mainly white) de Chatenoy, **Henry Pellé** and

Jean-Jacques Teiller.
Quincy (white) Jacques Rouzé.

Top Loire sweet wine vintages – With Chenin Blanc's acidity, these wines are amazingly age-worthy: 1947, 1949, 1959, 1962, 1969, 1971, 1976, 1983, 1985, 1988, 1989, 1990, 1995, 1996 and 1997.

THE RHÔNE VALLEY

This monster of a region has provided some of the best-value drinking wines of the last few years. Here, the Syrah, Grenache and Mourvèdre grape varieties rule the reds. The whites are commanded in the north by Viognier, and in the south by Roussanne and Marsanne. Spend some time here to get a comparison with what has happened in the New World. You will see that Shiraz (Syrah on holiday) is cropping up everywhere, producing everything from blockbuster reds to insipid alcoholic pretenders-to-the-throne. Then turn around, come back home to the Rhône and appreciate the great power, majesty and poise of these Old World originals.

THE NORTHERN RHÔNE (FROM NORTH TO SOUTH)

Côte Rôtie (red) Bernard Burgaud, Chapoutier, **Clusel-Roch £** (Les Grandes Places), Yves Cuilleron, **Pierre Gaillard £** (Rose Pourpre), **Yves Gangloff £**, Marius Gentaz-Dervieux, **E. Guigal £**, J.-P. & J.-L. Jamet and **René Rostaing £**.
Condrieu (white) **Yves Cuilleron £**, Christian Facchin, Pierre Gaillard, **E. Guigal £**, André Perret and Georges Vernay, **François Villard £**.
St-Joseph (red and white) **Jean-Louis Chave**, Yves Cuilleron,

Delas, Bernard Faurie, **Pierre Gaillard,** Pierre Gonon, Jean-Louis Grippat, André Perret.

Hermitage (red and white) **Chapoutier £**, **Jean-Louis Chave £**, Grippat, E. Guigal, **Paul Jaboulet Aîné £** (La Chapelle), Sorrel and **Tardieu-Laurent £**.

Crozes-Hermitage (mainly red) **Albert Belle**, Dumaine, **Alain Graillot**, Paul Jaboulet Aîné, Domaine Pochon (Curson) and **Gilles Robin**.

Cornas (red) **Thierry Allemand**, Auguste Clape, Jean Lionnet, Robert Michel, **Tunnel (Stéphane Robert)**, Noël Verset, **Tardieu-Laurent** and Alain Voge.

Top northern Rhône vintages – I prefer these Syrahs fairly young, although they can happily live up to twenty years: 1978, 1979, 1983, 1985, 1988, 1989, 1990, 1991, 1995, 1996, 1997, 1998, 1999 and 2000.

THE SOUTHERN RHÔNE
Côtes-du-Rhône (and **-Villages**) (red) **Clos Petite Bellane**, **Coudoulet de Beaucastel, des Espiers**, Domaine Gramenon, E. Guigal, Rayas (Fonsalette), Piaugier, **Marcel Richaud**, Tardieu-Laurent and Château du Trignon.

Lirac (red) A. & R. Maby and **de la Mordorée**.

Gigondas (red) Font-Sane, R. & J.-P. Meffre (Saint-Gayan), **Piaugier**, **Sainte-Cosme**, **Santa-Duc** and Château du Trignon.

Vacqueyras (red) **Emmanuel Reynaud**, **Château des Tours**.

Châteauneuf-du-Pape (red and white) **de Beaucastel**, Chapoutier, Charvin, **Clos du Caillou**, **Clos des Papes**, Fortia, de la Janasse, Marcoux, **de la Mordorée**, du Pégau, **Rayas**, Tardieu-Laurent and Versino.

Muscat de Beaumes-de-Venise (sweet white) Chapoutier, **Domaine de Durban** and Paul Jaboulet Aîné.

Top southern Rhône vintages – Again, I prefer these wines on the young side, but the best examples can last for up to thirty years: 1978, 1979, 1981, 1983, 1985, 1988, 1989, 1990, 1994, 1995, 1996, 1998, 1999 and 2000.

FRENCH COUNTRY
This is another huge, sprawling area to cover, which scoops together the rest of France's wine regions. I have picked out my favourite dry white, sweet white, red and fortified winemakers.

SOUTHWEST FRANCE
Bergerac (red and white) de la Jaubertie, **Moulin des Dames** and **La Tour des Gendres**.
Cahors (reds) **Châteaux du Cédre**, Lagrezette and Clos Triguedina.
Juraçon (dry and sweet whites) **Bellegarde**, **Cauhapé**, Clos Guirouilh, Clos Lapeyre and Clos Uroulat.
Madiran (reds) **d'Aydie**, **Bouscassé**, **Montus** and Domaine Pichard.
Monbazillac (sweet white) de l'Ancienne Cure, la Borderie and Tirecul La Gravière.
Saussignac (sweet white) Château Richard.

LANGUEDOC-ROUSSILLON
Banyuls (fortified) and **Collioure** (red) de la Casa Blanca, Château de Jau, **du Mas Blanc** and la Rectoire.
La Clape (red and white) Camplazens l'Hermitage, Domaine de

l'Hospitalet and Pech-Redon.

Corbières (mainly red) Etang des Colombes, de Lastours, **Château les Palais**, Pech-Latt and **Château Vaugélas**.

Costières de Nîmes (red, white and rosé) de Belle-Coste, **Grande-Cassagne**, Mourgues-du-Grès and **de Nages**.

Coteaux du Languedoc (red and white) **Les Aurelles**, de Font Caude, **Mas Jullien**, Puech-Haut, La Sauvagéonne and Abbaye de Valmagne.

Faugères (mainly red) **Alquier** and des Estanilles.

Minervois (red and white) **Borie de Maurel**, Clos Centeilles, Fabas, **de Gourgazaud** and d'Oupia.

Pic St-Loup (mainly red) Mas Bruguière, Cazeneuve, Ermitage du Pic St-Loup, **l'Hortus**, de Lascaux, Lascours and **Mas Mortiès**.

St-Chinian (red and white) Cazal Viel and Coujan.

Miscellaneous estates of excellence (and where to find them): **Mas Amiel** – Maury; **Domaine de Baruel** – Cévennes; **Clos Bellevue** – Muscat de Lunel; **Cazes** – Muscat de Rivesaltes; **Mas de Daumas Gassac** – L'Herault; **Granges des Pères** – L'Herault; **Domaine de Ravanès** – Coteaux de Murveil; and **Elian da Ros** – Côtes du Marmandais.

PROVENCE

Bandol (red) Pradeaux, **de la Bégude**, Château Jean-Pierre Gaussen, **Lafran-Veyrolles**, **Tempier**, de Pibarnon, Mas de la Rouvière and La Suffrène.

Les Baux-de-Provence (mainly red) Hauvette, des Terres Blanches and **de Trévallon £**.

Bellet (red, white and rosé) Château de Crémat.

Cassis (mainly white) **Clos Ste-Madeleine**.
Côtes de Provence (mainly red) Domaine de Rimauresq,
Domaine Gavoty, Domaine de St-Baillon and **Domaine de la Courtade**.
Palette (red, white and rosé) Château Simone

GERMANY

My German list is packed with superstars. Find one of these producer's wines on a list and you are guaranteed wonderful drinking. The main grape to explore is Riesling. Follow its range of styles from bone dry and refreshing, to unctuous and pudding-friendly. The best producers are: J.B. Becker, Dr Bürklin-Wolf, J.J. Cristoffel, Fritz Haag, Weingut Kerpen, von Kesselstatt, Koehler-Ruprecht, **Franz Künstler**, H. & R. Lingenfelder, Schloss Lieser, Dr Loosen, **Egon Müller**, Müller-Cattoir, **J.J. Prüm**, Willi Schaefer, von Schubert-Maximin Grünhaus, **Selbach-Oster** and Dr H. Thanisch.

Top German vintages – Riesling loves the long haul: 1971, 1975, 1976, 1983, 1985, 1988, 1989, 1990, 1992, 1993, 1995, 1996, 1997, 1998, 1999 and 2000.

GREAT BRITAIN

Support your local wine industry. Here is a short list of our best home-grown stars – Bruisyard, Camel Valley, **Chapel Down**, **Davenport**, Denbies, Nyetimber, Ridgeview, Sharpham, Shawsgate, **Three Choirs** and Valley Vineyards.

ITALY

A minefield of regions, grape varieties and styles of wine, but if you stick to the estates below, you will hit upon some celestial offerings.

NORTHWEST
PIEDMONT
Barolo, Barbaresco and other reds – **Elio Altare**, Bruno Ceretto, **Aldo Conterno**, Giacomo Conterno, Domenico Clerico, Fontanafredda, **Angelo Gaja £**, Giuseppe Mascarello, **Luciano Sandrone**, Paolo Scavino, La Spinetta and **Roberto Voerzio**. Moscato (fizzy sweet white) **Fontanafredda** and **La Spinetta**. Gavi (dry white) Nicola Bergaglio, **La Giustiniana** and La Scolca. Arneis (dry white) Bric Cenciurio and Carlo Deltetto.

LOMBARDY
Red and white – Bellavista, **Ca' del Bosco**, **Ca' dei Frati** and Nino Negri.

Top Piedmont vintages – The Nebbiolo grape's structure and tannin carries these wines far: 1970, 1971, 1974, 1978, 1982, 1985, 1988, 1989, 1990, 1995, 1996, 1997, 1998 and 1999.

NORTHEAST
TRENTINO
All styles – **Vigneto Dalzocchio**, **Foradori**, Bossi Fedrigotti, Ferrari, Letrari, Pojer & Sandri and **Tenuta San Leonardo**.

ALTO ADIGE
All styles – **Colterenzio**, San Michele Appiano, Hofstätter, **Franz Haas** and Alois Lageder.

VENETO
Soave (white) **Roberto Anselmi**, **Ca' Rugate**, Gini and **Leonildo Pieropan**.

Valpolicella (red) **Allegrini**, Dal Forno, Masi and **Giuseppe Quintarelli £**.

Miscellaneous estates of excellence: (fizz) – Ruggeri and (reds and sweeties) – Maculan.

Top vintages for Amarone della Valpolicella – The power in Amarone makes these wines long-lived: 1970, 1971, 1974, 1976, 1979, 1983, 1985, 1988, 1990, 1993, 1995, 1997, 1998, 1999 and 2000.

FRIULI VENEZIA GIULIA
All styles – Livio Felluga, **Vinnaioli Jermann**, Miani, **Alvararo Pecorari**, **Vittorio & Giovanni Puiatti**, Ronco del Gnemiz, Mario Schiopetto, Tercic and Villa Russiz.

CENTRAL
TUSCANY
Chianti (red) P. Antinori, Brolio, Villa Caffagio, **Carobbio**, **Castello di Fonterutoli**, **Isole e Olena**, **Felsina Berardenga**, Fontodi, **Selvapiana** and **Querciabella**.
Brunello di Montalcino (red) Altesino, **Argiano**, Case Basse, **Costanti**, La Gerla, Lisini and Silvio Nardi.
Vino Nobile di Montepulciano (red) **Dei**, Il Macchione and **Poliziano**.
Carmignano (red) Ambra and **Tenuta di Capezzana**.
Super-Tuscans (red) **Ardingo** (Calbello), Campora (Falchini), **Il Carbonaione** (Poggio Scalette), **Cepparello £** (Isole e Olena), Cortaccio (Villa Caffagio), Flaccianello della Pieve (Fontodi), Fontalloro (Felsina Berardenga), Ghiaie della Furba (Capezzana), Lupicaia (Tenuta del Terricio), **Ornellaia £** (L. Antinori), Palazzo Altesi (Altesino), Paleo

Rosso (Le Macchiole), **Saffredi £** (Le Pupille), Sammarco (Castello dei Rampolla), **Sassicaia £** (Marchesi Incisa della Rochetta), Solaia (P. Antinori), **Solengo £** (Argiano), Tassinaia (Tenuta del Terriccio) and Tignanello (P. Antinori).

Vernaccia di San Gimignano (white) Montenidoli, Pietraserena and Teruzzi & Puthod.

Vin Santo (sweetie) **Isole e Olena £**, Selvapiana and Villa Branca.

Top Tuscan vintages – I usually attack these wines early – within ten years – although they seem to be able to hang on for ages: 1975, 1978, 1979, 1982, 1983, 1985, 1988, 1990, 1993, 1995, 1997, 1998, 1999 and 2000.

MARCHE
Red and white – **Coroncino**, Brunori, Saladini Pilastri and **Umani Ronchi**.

UMBRIA
Red and white – Bigi, **Arnaldo Caprai**, Castello della Sala, **Lungarotti** and Palazzone.

LAZIO
Red and white – **Castel De Paolis**, Falesco and Pallavincini.

ABRUZZO AND MOLISE
Red and white – Di Majo Norante and **Edoardo Valentini**.

SOUTHERN AND ISLANDS
A handful of producers whose reds and whites are worth tracking down.

Puglia – Botromagno, Francesco Candido and **Cosimo Taurino**.
Campania – Feudi di San Gregorio, Mastroberardino and **Montevetrano**.
Basilicata – D'Angelo and **Paternoster**.
Calabria – Librandi and San Francesco.
Sicily – De Bartoli, Inycon and **Planeta**.
Sardinia – Antonio Argiolas, Sella & Mosca and **Santadi**.

NEW ZEALAND

New Zealand wines just get better every year. The list below would only have been half as long two years ago. You can now drink excellent Chardonnay and Cabernet Sauvignon, as well as the more renowned Sauvignon Blanc and Pinot Noir. This country continues its meteoric rise. The top producers are – **Ata Rangi**, **Cloudy Bay**, Collards, **Dry River**, **Esk Valley**, **Felton Road**, Giesen Estate, Goldwater Estate, Grove Mill, Hawkesbridge, **Hunter's**, **Isabel Estate**, **Jackson Estate**, Kim Crawford, **Kumeu River**, Lawson's Dry Hills, Martinborough Vineyards, Palliser Estate, Selaks, Seresin Estate, Solstone, Te Mata, Tohu, Vavasour, Vidal, Villa Maria and **Wither Hills**.

Top New Zealand red vintages – Almost always drunk young, few reds would last more than ten years: 1989, 1991, 1994, 1995, 1996, 1998, 1999 and 2000.

PORTUGAL

Portugal makes two of the finest fortified wines in the world – port and Madeira. There are only a few top producers in each region, so this is an easy one. The still wine side of things is enjoying a massive expansion period and things are starting to get exciting.

PORT

The best port houses are – **Dow**, **Fonseca**, **Graham**, **Quinta do Noval Nacional**, **Taylor** and **Warre**.

Top Port vintages – No surprise, port is the keeper of them all: 1927, 1931, 1935, 1945, 1948, 1955, 1963, 1966, 1970, 1977, 1980, 1983, 1985, 1992, 1994 and 1997.

MADEIRA

The best producers are – **Blandy's**, **Cossart Gordon** and Henriques & Henriques.

THE REST OF PORTUGAL

Here's a short list of the commendable winemakers in the better regions.

Alentejo Quinta do Carmo and **Segada**.
Bairrada Caves São João and Luis Pato.
Dão **Quinta dos Roques**, José-Maria da Fonseca and Conde de Santar.
Douro **Quinta do Crasto**, Quinta de Gaivosa, **Quinta do Portal**, **Quinta de Roriz**, Quinta de la Rosa and Quinta do Vale da Raposa.
Estremadura Quinta da Boavista, Quinta de Pancas and Palha Canas.
Ribatejo Bright Brothers.
Setúbal José-Maria da Fonseca.
Terras do Sado Quinta de Camarate, Pasmados, Periquita and João Pires.
Vinho Verde Palácio da Brejoeira.

SOUTH AFRICA

An astonishing performance over the last few years has catapulted
South African wines into my cellar (gently). I have nothing but
admiration for the speed in which this country has got its wines on
track to compete with the rest of the world. The line-up of estates
below has no wines over £25, so there are no **£**. My problem has
been choosing favourites, as they are all seemingly worthy of **bold**
type. Choose any of the wines made by any of these estates and
you should, I hope, be impressed at not only the taste, but also the
value for money. The wine producers – Beaumont, Beyerskloof,
Boekenhoutskloof, **Bouchard Finlayson**, Fairview, Grangehurst,
Hamilton Russell (and Ashbourne), Hartenberg, Hidden Valley,
Jean Daneel, **Jordan**, Kanonkop, **Klein Constantia**, Linton Park,
Longridge, Morgenhof, Neethlingshof, **Neil Ellis**, Simonsig, Spice
Route, Steenberg, Stellenzicht, **Thelema Mountain**, Veenwouden,
Vergelegen, Villiera, **Warwick**, **Whalehaven** and Wildekrans.

Top South African vintages – It's rare to find older examples, and
there is not much variation year on year from the best producers
due to largely uniform weather conditions: 1986, 1987, 1989, 1991,
1992, 1994, 1995, 1997, 1998 and 2000.

SPAIN

Here I have only noted my favourite regions, and within each one,
my top producers. Spain is woefully underrated at present and there is
some delightful bargain drinking to be had. Almost all of the wineries
below make great red wines, only a handful make whites to match.
Campo de Borja Bodegas Borsao.
Calatayud Marqués de Aragón.

Chacolí de Guetaria Txomín Etaniz.

Conca de Barberá Josep Foraster.

Jerez (sherry) González Byass, **Lustau** and **Valdespino**.

Navarra Agramont, Guelbenzu, **Navasqüés**, Ochoa and Principe de Viana.

Penedès Can Rafols dels Caus, Jean Léon, Puig & Roca and **Miguel Torres**.

Priorato Clos de l'Obac, Clos Martinet, **René Barbier (Clos Mogador)** £ and Scala Dei.

Rías Baixas Lagar de Cervera, **Pazo de Barrantes** and Valdamor.

Ribera del Duero **Cillar de Silos**, Pago de Carraovejas, **Pesquera**, Tarsus and **Vega Sicilia £**.

Rioja Barón de Ley, **CVNE**, Dominio de Montalvo, López De Heredia, Marqués de Murrieta, Muga, Navajas, **Remelluri**, **La Rioja Alta**, Salceda, Urbina and **Marqués de Vargas**.

Somontano Viñas del Vero (Blecua).

Tarragona Capçanes and **Laurona**.

Terra Alta Xavier Clua and Bárbara Forès.

Toro Viña Bajoz.

Top Rioja vintages – I like to drink Riojas when they still have a lot of fruit, generally within ten years: 1978, 1981, 1982, 1985, 1987, 1989, 1990, 1991, 1994, 1995 and 1996.

USA
CALIFORNIA

This represents an enormous industry with thousands of producers, so how can I sort it all out? By grape variety, of course. So find your favourite grape, and choose from the wineries listed.

Cabernet Sauvignon/Merlot/Cabernet Franc Beringer, **Bryant Family £**, Caymus, Clos LaChance, Corison, Dalle Valle, Dominus, **Etude £**, Forman, Gallo Estate, **Harlan Estate £**, **Havens**, Paul Hobbs, Justin Vineyards, Lail Vineyards, Matanzas Creek, Robert Mondavi, Moraga, Newton, **Paradigm £**, Joseph Phelps, Quintessa, **Ridge £**, **Shafer £**, **Spottswoode £**, **Stag's Leap £** and **Viader £**.

Chardonnay Arrowood, **Au Bon Climat**, Beringer, Clos LaChance, Gallo Estate, Paul Hobbs, **Kistler £**, **Matanzas Creek**, Robert Mondavi, Sinskey and **Shafer £**.

Sauvignon Blanc Beringer, **Carmenet**, Matanzas Creek and Robert Mondavi.

Pinot Noir Au Bon Climat, **Calera £**, **Etude £**, **Kistler £**, Saintsbury and Talley Vineyards.

Rhône Rangers Au Bon Climat, Bonny Doon, **Jade Mountain**, Qupé, **Sean Thackrey** and **Turley £**.

Zinfandel Cline, **Elyse**, De Loach, **Doug Nalle**, Ravenswood, **Renwood, Ridge** and Turley.

Inexpensive estates: Bonny Doon, **Cartlidge & Browne**, Fetzer Bonterra, **Marietta Cellars**, R.H. Phillips, **Ramsay** and Wente.

Top Californian vintages – These wines don't offer the longevity that you might expect, as they generally mature early: 1984, 1985, 1986, 1987, 1990, 1991, 1992, 1994, 1995, 1997, 1998, 1999 and 2000.

PACIFIC NORTHWEST
Still hard to get hold of, and invariably dear, the wines from Washington State and Oregon are eclectic and tend only to be worth it when you are feeling inquisitive.

Oregon's best estates Adelsheim, Bethel Heights, **Cristom**, Domaine Drouhin, Duck Pond, **Evesham Wood**, Ponzi and Rex Hill. **Washington State's best estates** L'Ecole No 41, **Château Ste-Michelle**, **Leonetti**, **Andrew Will £** and Woodward Canyon.

Top Oregon and Washington vintages: 1989, 1990, 1991, 1992, 1994, 1996, 1997, 1998, 1999 and 2000.

THE REST OF THE OLD WORLD

Hungary's decadent sweet wine Tokaji, is a cross between Sauternes and a top-flight sherry – see the Top 250 for two fine examples. **Lebanon** has one great wine, **Château Musar**. **Greek** wines are all the rage and look to my Top 250 to see if any have made it.

DIRECTORY
OF UK WINE
MERCHANTS

If retail therapy is an enjoyable pastime, then buying wine must be its indulgent peak. And in order for you to experience this pleasure fully, you must understand the complexities of the vast UK wine market. I have compiled a large directory of independent wine merchants (sorted alphabetically and regionally), supermarkets and wine specific chain stores. I have included the main contact number for each company's HQ. Use it. If you want to ask about a wine that they stock, phone to check that it is available before setting out. Better still, arrange for delivery of the wine to avoid lugging heavy cases around. Every outlet mentioned below delivers wine around the country. Many of these companies have newsletters (either via email or post), so ask to be put on their mailing list and you will be first to hear about new releases. And most importantly of all, if you find an independent wine merchant near to where you live, support them. They are the lifeblood of diversity and eclecticism in our market.

Supermarkets and chain stores are fabulous and are improving their selections every day. There has never been a better time to shop for wine in a supermarket. Wine store chains are always locked in battle, endeavouring to sniff out better wines than the opposition. And, we, the customers are the inevitable winners. But 'indies' are there to enable you to pursue your favourite regions to a conclusion, for you to buy the one-off wine of your dreams and for you to broaden your horizons and wander 'off piste' into new uncharted territories. In the same way that your local butcher and fishmonger know your likes and dislikes, your local wine merchant will get to know your taste. Now what could be better than that?

RECOMMENDED LARGER CHAIN STORES AND SUPERMARKETS (PLUS ABBREVIATIONS)

Asda (**Asd**) 243 stores 0113 243 5435 ✪

E.H. Booth & Co., of Lancashire, Cheshire, Cumbria and Yorkshire (**Boo**) 25 stores 01772 251701 ✪

Co-operative Group CWS (**Coo**) 1,100 stores 0800 068 6727

First Quench – including Bottoms Up (**Bot**), Thresher (**Thr**), Victoria Wine (**Vic**) and Wine Rack (**WRa**) 2,400 stores 01707 387200 ✪

Majestic Wine Warehouses (**Maj**) 95 stores 01923 298200 ✪ C

Marks & Spencer (**M&S**) 305 stores 020 7935 4422 ✪

Wm Morrison (**Mor**) 110 stores 01924 870000

Nicolas UK of London 25 stores 020 8964 5469

Oddbins (**Odd**) 240 stores and Oddbins Fine Wine shops (**OFW**) 7 stores 020 8944 4400 ✪

Safeway (**Saf**) 478 stores 020 8848 8744 ✪

Sainsbury's (**Sai**) 439 stores 0800 636262 ✪

Somerfield Stores (**Som**) 400 stores 0117 935 6669

Tesco Stores (**Tes**) 640 stores 0800 505555 ✪

Unwins Ltd (**Unw**) 451 stores 01322 272711 ✪

Waitrose (**Wai**) 137 stores 01344 825232 ✪

Wine Cellar (**WCe**) 60 stores 0800 838251

RECOMMENDED INDEPENDENT RETAIL SPECIALISTS, SMALL CHAINS, WINE BROKERS AND MAIL ORDER WINE COMPANIES
SORTED ALPHABETICALLY

A & A Wines, Cranleigh, Surrey 01483 274666 C
A & B Vintners, Brenchley, Kent 01892 724977 ✪ M C
Adnams Wine Merchants, Southwold, Suffolk 01502 727251 ✪
Ameys Wines, Sudbury, Suffolk 01787 377144
Amps Fine Wines of Oundle, near Peterborough, Northamptonshire
   01832 273502
Arkells Vintners, Swindon, Wiltshire 01793 823026
John Armit Wines, London 020 7908 0600 ✪ M C F
W.J. Armstrong, East Grinstead, West Sussex 01342 321478
Arnolds, Broadway, Worcestershire 01386 852427
Arriba Kettle & Co., Honeybourne, Worcestershire 01386 833024 C
Australian Wine Club, Hounslow, Middlesex 0800 8562004 ✪ M C
Averys, Bristol 0117 921 4146

Bacchanalia, Cambridge 01223 576292
Ballantynes, Cowbridge, Vale of Glamorgan 01446 774840 ✪
Balls Brothers, London 020 7739 1642 M C
Georges Barbier, London 020 8852 8501 ✪ M C
Barrels & Bottles, Sheffield 0114 255 6611
Bat & Bottle, Knightley, Staffordshire 01785 284495
Beaconsfield Wine Cellar, Beaconsfield, Buckinghamshire 01494
   675545

Beaminster Fine Wines, Beaminster, Dorset 01308 862350

Bennetts Fine Wines, Chipping Campden, Gloucestershire
01386 840392 ✪

Bentalls, Kingston-upon-Thames, Surrey 020 8546 1001

Bergerac Wine Cellar, St Helier, Jersey 01534 870756

Berkmann Wine Cellars, London 020 7609 4711 ✪M

Berry Bros. & Rudd, London 0870 900 4300 ✪F

Bibendum Wine Ltd, London 020 7916 7706 ✪M C F

Bideford Wines, Bideford, Devon 01237 470507

Booths of Stockport, Heaton Moor, Stockport 0161 432 3309

Bordeaux Index, London 020 7278 9495 ✪M F

The Bottleneck, Broadstairs, Kent 01843 861095

Brinkleys Wines, London 020 7351 1683

F.E. Brown & Son, Hoddesdon, Hertfordshire 01992 421327 M C

Burgundy Shuttle, London 020 7341 4053 M C

Butlers Wine Cellar, Brighton, East Sussex 01273 698724 ✪

Anthony Byrne Fine Wines, Ramsey, Cambridgeshire
01487 814555 M C

D. Byrne & Co., Clitheroe, Lancashire 01200 423152 ✪

Cairns & Hickey, Bramhope, Leeds 0113 267 3746

Carley & Webb, Framlingham, Suffolk 01728 723503

Carringtons, Manchester 0161 881 0099

Castang Wine Shippers, Pelynt, Cornwall 01503 220359 M C

Les Caves du Patron, Stoneygate, Leicester 0116 221 8221

Andrew Chapman Fine Wines, Abingdon, Oxfordshire
0845 458 0707

The Charterhouse Wine Co., London 020 7587 1302

Cheshire Smokehouse, Wilmslow, Cheshire 01625 540123

Chippendale Fine Wines, Bradford, West Yorkshire
  01274 582424 **M C**
Classic Wines, Chester, Cheshire 01244 288444
Clifton Cellars, Bristol 0117 973 0287
Brian Coad Fine Wines, Ivybridge, Devon 01752 896545 **M C**
Cochonnet Wines, Falmouth, Cornwall 01326 340332
Cockburns, Leith, Edinburgh 0131 346 1113
Colombier Vins Fins, Swadlincote, Derbyshire
  01283 552552 **M C**
Connollys, Birmingham 0121 236 9269
Corks, Cotham, Bristol 0117 973 1620
Corkscrew Wines, Carlisle, Cumbria 01228 543033
Corney & Barrow, London 020 7539 3200 ✪ **F**
Croque-en-Bouche, Malvern Wells, Worcestershire
  01684 565612 ✪ **M C**

Dartmouth Vintners, Dartmouth, Devon 01803 832602
Decorum Vintners, London 020 7589 6755 ✪ **M C**
deFINE Food and Wine, Sandiway, Cheshire 01606 882101
Rodney Densem Wines, Nantwich, Cheshire 01270 626999
Direct Wine Shipments, Belfast, Northern Ireland
  028 9050 8000 ✪
Direct Wines, Windsor 0870 444 8383 **M C**
Domaine Direct, London 020 7837 1142 ✪ **C**
The Dorchester Wine Centre at Eldridge Pope, Dorchester,
  Dorset 01305 258266 ✪
Draycott Wines, Topsham, Devon 01392 874501
Dunnells Ltd, St Peter Port, Guernsey 01534 736418
Du Vin, Henley-on-Thames, Oxfordshire 01491 637888

Edencroft Fine Wines, Nantwich, Cheshire 01270 629975
Ben Ellis, Brockham, Surrey 01737 842160 ✪ C
El Vino, London 020 7353 5384
English Wine Centre, Alfriston Roundabout, East Sussex
    01323 870164
Eton Vintners, Windsor 01753 790188 M
Evertons, Ombersley, Worcestershire 01905 620282
Evingtons Wine Merchants, Leicester 0116 254 2702

Farr Vintners, London 020 7821 2000 ✪ M F
Fine & Rare Wines, London 020 8960 1995 ✪ M F
Fine Cheese Co., Bath 01225 483407
Irma Fingal-Rock, Monmouth, Monmouthshire 01600 712372
Le Fleming Wines, Harpenden, Hertfordshire 01582 760125 M C
La Forge Wines, Marksbury, Bath 01761 472349
Fortnum & Mason, London 020 7734 8040 ✪
Four Walls Wine Company, Chilgrove, West Sussex
    01243 535360 ✪ M F
Friarwood, London 020 7736 2628

Gallery Wines, Gomshall, Surrey 01483 203795
Garland Wine Cellar, Ashtead, Surrey 01372 275247
Garrards, Cockermouth, Cumbria 01900 823592
Gauntleys, Nottingham 0115 911 0555
General Wine Company, Liphook, Hampshire 01428 727744 ✪
Glumangate Wines, Chesterfield, Derbyshire 01246 200499
Goedhuis & Co., London 020 7793 7900 ✪ M C F
Peter Graham Wines, Norwich, Norfolk 01603 625657

Great Gaddesden Wines, Harpenden, Hertfordshire
01582 760606 **M C**
Great Northern Wine Company, Ripon, North Yorkshire
01765 606767 **M**
Great Western Wine Company, Bath 01225 322800
Peter Green, Edinburgh 0131 229 5925
The Grog Blossom, London 020 7794 7808
Patrick Grubb Selections, Oxford 01869 340229 ✪
Gunson Fine Wines, South Godstone, Surrey
01342 843974 ✪ **M C**

H & H Bancroft, London 0870 4441700 ✪ **M C**
Handford – Holland Park, London 020 7221 9614 ✪
Hanslope Wines, Milton Keynes, Buckinghamshire
01908 510262
Roger Harris Wines, Weston Longville, Norfolk
01603 880171 ✪ **M C**
Harrods, London 020 7730 1324
John Harvey & Sons, Bristol 0117 927 5006 **M C**
Harvey Nichols & Co., London 020 7201 8537 ✪
Richard Harvey Wines, Wareham, Dorset 01929 481437 **M C**
The Haslemere Cellar, Haslemere, Surrey 01428 645081 ✪
Haynes, Hanson & Clark, London 020 7259 0102 and Stow-on-the-Wold, Gloucestershire 01451 870808 ✪
Hedley Wright, Bishop's Stortford, Hertfordshire 01279 465818 **C**
Pierre Henck, Wolverhampton, West Midlands
01902 751022 **M C**
Charles Hennings Vintners, Pulborough, West Sussex
01798 872485

George Hill, Loughborough, Leicestershire 01509 212717
Hopton Wines, Kidderminster, Worcestershire
01299 270734 **M C**
Hoults Wine Merchants, Huddersfield, West Yorkshire
01484 510700
House of Townend, Kingston upon Hull, East Yorkshire
01482 586582
Ian G. Howe, Newark, Nottinghamshire 01636 704366
Victor Hugo Wines, St Saviour, Jersey 01534 507977

Inspired Wines, Cleobury Mortimer, Shropshire 01299 270064
Inverarity Vaults, Biggar 01899 308000
Irvine Robertson, Edinburgh 0131 553 3521 **C**

Jeroboams (incorporating **Laytons Wine Merchants**),
London 020 7259 6716 ✪
Michael Jobling, Newcastle-upon-Tyne 0191 261 5298 **M C**
The Jolly Vintner, Tiverton, Devon 01884 255644
L & F Jones, Radstock near Bath 01761 417117
S.H. Jones, Banbury, Oxfordshire 01295 251179
Justerini & Brooks, London 020 7484 6400 ✪
Just in Case Wine Merchants, Bishop's Waltham, Hampshire
01489 892969

Joseph Keegan, Holyhead, Isle of Anglesey 01407 762333
John Kelly Wines, Boston Spa, West Yorkshire
01937 842965 **M C**
David Kibble Wines, Fontwell, West Sussex 01243 544111
Richard Kihl, Aldeburgh, Suffolk 01728 454455 ✪ **F C**

✪ = Jukesy-rated wine merchant worthy of particular note
C = Wine sold by the case (often mixed) of twelve bottles

Laithwaites, Reading, Berkshire 0870 444 8282 M C
Lay & Wheeler, Colchester, Essex 01206 764446
Laymont & Shaw, Truro, Cornwall 01872 270545 M C
Lea & Sandeman, London 020 7244 5200 ✪
Liberty Wines, London 020 7720 5350 ✪ M C
O.W. Loeb, London 020 7928 7750 ✪ M C
J & H Logan, Edinburgh 0131 667 2855
Longford Wines, Lewes, East Sussex 01273 400012 M C
Luckins Wine Store, Great Dunmow, Essex 01371 872839

Martinez Fine Wines, Ilkley, West Yorkshire 01943 603241 ✪
Mill Hill Wines, London 020 8959 6754
Mills Whitcombe, Lower Maescoed, Herefordshire
  01873 860222 C
Milton Sandford Wines, Knowl Hill, Berkshire
  01628 829449 ✪ M C
Mitchells Wine Merchants, Sheffield 0114 274 5587
Montrachet Fine Wines, London 020 7928 1990 ✪ M C
Moreno Wine, London 020 7286 0678 ✪
Morris & Verdin, London 020 7357 8866 ✪ M C

James Nicholson, Crossgar, Co. Down, Northern Ireland
  028 4483 0091 ✪
Nickolls & Perks, Stourbridge, West Midlands 01384 394518
Noble Rot Wine Warehouse, Bromsgrove, Worcestershire
  01527 575606
The Nobody Inn, Doddiscombsleigh, Devon 01647 252394 ✪

Oasis Wines, Southend-on-Sea, Essex 01702 293999

The Old Forge Wine Cellar, Storrington, West Sussex
01903 744246
Oxford Wine Company, Witney, Oxfordshire 01865 301144 ✪

Thomas Panton, Tetbury, Gloucestershire 01666 503088 M
Paxton & Whitfield, London 020 7930 0259
Thos Peatling, Bury St Edmunds, Suffolk 01284 714285
Peckham & Rye, Glasgow 0141 445 4555 ✪
Penistone Court Wine Cellars, Penistone, Sheffield
01226 766037 M C
Philglas & Swiggot, London 020 7924 4494 ✪
Christopher Piper Wines, Ottery St Mary, Devon
01404 814139 ✪
Terry Platt Wine Merchants, Llandudno, Conwy
01492 874099 ✪ M C
Playford Ros, Thirsk, North Yorkshire 01845 526777 M C
Portal, Dingwall & Norris, Emsworth, Hampshire 01243 377883
Portland Wine Co., Sale, Manchester 0161 962 8752

Quay West Wines, Stoke Canon, Exeter 01392 841833 C
Quellyn Roberts, Chester, Cheshire 01244 310455

R.S. Wines, Bristol 0117 963 1780 M C
Arthur Rackham, Guildford, Surrey 01483 722962 C
Raeburn Fine Wines, Edinburgh 0131 554 2652 ✪
Ravensbourne Wine, London 020 8692 9655 C
Reid Wines, Hallatrow, Bristol 01761 452645 ✪ M F
La Réserve, London 020 7589 2020 ✪
Revelstoke Wines, London 020 8875 0077 ✪ M C

Howard Ripley, London 020 8360 0020 and 020 8877 3065 **M C**
Roberson, London 020 7371 2121 ✿
Roberts & Speight, Beverley, East Yorkshire 01482 870717
Robert Rolls, London 020 7606 1166 ✿**M C F**

St Martin Vintners, Brighton, East Sussex 01273 777788
Sandhams Wine Merchants, Caistor, Lincolnshire 01472 852118
Scatchard, Liverpool 0151 709 7073
Seckford Wines, Woodbridge, Suffolk 01394 446622 ✿**M C F**
Selfridges, London 020 7318 3730 and Manchester
0161 629 1234 ✿
Shaftesbury Fine Wines, Shaftesbury, Dorset 01747 850059
Shaws, Beaumaris, Isle of Anglesey 01248 810328
Edward Sheldon, Shipston-on-Stour, Warwickshire
01608 661409
Laurence Smith, Edinburgh 0131 667 3327 **M C**
Soho Wine Supply, London 020 7636 8490
The Sommelier Wine Co., St Peter Port, Guernsey
01481 721677 ✿
Springfield Wines, near Huddersfield, West Yorkshire
01484 864929
Frank Stainton Wines, Kendal, Cumbria 01539 731886
William Stedman, Caerleon, Newport 01633 430055
Charles Steevenson, Tavistock, Devon 01822 616272 **M C**
Stevens Garnier, Oxford 01865 263303

T & W Wines, Thetford, Norfolk 01842 765646
Tanners, Shrewsbury, Shropshire 01743 234455 ✿
Totnes Wine Co., Totnes, Devon 01803 866357

Trenchermans, Sherborne, Dorset 01935 432857
Turville Valley Wines, Great Missenden, Buckinghamshire
01494 868818 ✪ **M C F**

Uncorked, London 020 7638 5998

Valvona & Crolla, Edinburgh 0131 556 6066 ✪
Helen Verdcourt, Maidenhead, Berkshire 01628 625577 **M C**
La Vigneronne, London 020 7589 6113 ✪
Villeneuve Wines, Peebles, Haddington and Edinburgh
01721 722500 ✪
Vin du Van, Appledore, Kent 01233 758727 ✪ **M C**
Vinceremos, Leeds 0113 205 4545 **M C**
The Vine Trail, Hotwells, Bristol 0117 921 1770 ✪ **M C**
The Vineyard, Dorking, Surrey 01306 876828
Vino Vino, New Malden, Surrey 07703 436949 **M C**
The Vintage House, London 020 7437 2592
Vintage Roots, Arborfield, Berkshire 0118 976 1999 **M**

Waterloo Wine, London 020 7403 7967
Waters Wine Merchants, Coventry, Warwick 01926 888889
David J. Watt Fine Wines, Ashby-de-la-Zouch, Leicestershire
01530 415704 shop, 01530 413953 **M**
Weavers, Nottingham, Nottinghamshire 0115 958 0922
Wessex Wines, Bridport, Dorset 01308 427177 **C**
Whitebridge Wines, Stone, Staffordshire 01785 817229
Whitesides, Clitheroe, Lancashire 01200 422281
Whittalls Wines, Walsall, West Midlands 01922 636161 **C**
Wilkinson Vintners, London 020 7272 1982 ✪ **M C F**

James Williams, Narberth, Pembrokeshire 01834 862200
Willoughbys the Wine Merchants, Manchester 0161 834 6850
Wimbledon Wine Cellar, London 020 8540 9979 ✪
Winchcombe Wine Merchants, Winchcombe, Gloucestershire
   01242 604313
The Wine Cellar, Croydon, Greater London 020 8657 6936
Wine Society, Stevenage, Hertfordshire 01438 741177 ✪ M C F
The Wine Treasury, London 020 7793 9999 ✪ M C
The Winery, London 020 7286 6475 ✪ F
Wines of Interest, Ipswich, Suffolk 01473 215752
The Winesmith, Peterborough, Cambridgeshire 01780 783102
WineTime, Milnthorpe, Cumbria 01539 562030 M C
Woodhouse Wines, Blandford, Dorset 01258 452141
The Wright Wine Company, Skipton, North Yorkshire
   01756 700886 ✪
Wrightson & Co. Wine Merchants, Darlington
   01325 374134 M C
Wycombe Wines, High Wycombe, Buckinghamshire
   01494 437228
Peter Wylie Fine Wines, Plymtree, Devon 01884 277555 ✪ F

Yapp Brothers, Mere, Wiltshire 01747 860423 ✪ M C
Noel Young Wines, Trumpington, Cambridgeshire
   01223 844744 ✪

M = Mail order company, usually with no retail premises
F = Fine wine sales/wine broker/good range of expensive stuff!

RECOMMENDED INDEPENDENT RETAIL SPECIALISTS, SMALL CHAINS, WINE BROKERS AND MAIL ORDER WINE COMPANIES
SORTED REGIONALLY

LONDON

John Armit Wines, W11 020 7908 0600 ✪ M C F
Balls Brothers, E2 020 7739 1642 M C
Georges Barbier, SE12 020 885 28501 ✪ M C
Berkmann Wine Cellars, N7 020 7609 4711 ✪ M
Berry Bros. & Rudd, SW1 0870 900 4300 ✪ F
Bibendum Wine Ltd, NW1 020 7916 7706 ✪ M C F
Bordeaux Index, EC1 020 7278 9495 ✪ M F
Brinkleys Wines, SW10 020 7351 1683
Burgundy Shuttle, SW11 020 7341 4053 M C
Australian Wine Club, Hounslow 0800 856 2004 ✪ M C
The Charterhouse Wine Co., SE11 020 7587 1302
Corney & Barrow, EC1 020 7539 3200 ✪ F
Decorum Vintners, SW7 020 7589 6755 ✪ M C
Domaine Direct, N1 020 7837 1142 ✪ C
El Vino, EC4 020 7353 5384
Farr Vintners, SW1 020 7821 2000 ✪ M F
Fine & Rare Wines, W10 020 8960 1995 ✪ M F
Fortnum & Mason, W1 020 7734 8040 ✪
Friarwood, SW6 020 7736 2628
Goedhuis & Co., SW8 020 7793 7900 ✪ M C F
The Grog Blossom, NW6 020 7794 7808

✪ = Jukesy-rated wine merchant worthy of particular note
C = Wine sold by the case (often mixed) of twelve bottles

H & H Bancroft, SW8 0870 444 1700 ✪ M C
Handford – Holland Park, W11 020 7221 9614 ✪
Harrods, SW1 020 7730 1324
Harvey Nichols & Co., SW1 020 7201 8537 ✪
Haynes, Hanson & Clark, SW1 020 7259 0102 ✪
Jeroboams (incorporating Laytons Wine Merchants), W1
    020 7259 6716 ✪
Justerini & Brooks, SW1 020 7484 6400 ✪
Lea & Sandeman, SW10 020 7244 5200 ✪
Liberty Wines, SW8 020 7720 5350 ✪ M C
O.W. Loeb, SE1 020 7928 7750 ✪ M C
Mill Hill Wines, NW7 020 8959 6754
Montrachet Fine Wines, SE1 020 7928 1990 ✪ M C
Moreno Wine, W9 020 7286 0678 ✪
Morris & Verdin, SE1 020 7357 8866 ✪ M C
Nicolas UK of London 25 stores 020 8964 5469
Paxton & Whitfield, SW1 020 7930 0259
Philglas & Swiggot, SW11 020 7924 4494 ✪
Ravensbourne Wine, SE10 020 8692 9655 C
La Réserve, SW3 020 7589 2020 ✪
Revelstoke Wines, SW15 020 8875 0077 ✪ M C
Howard Ripley, N21 020 8360 0020 and 020 8877 3065 M C
Roberson, W14 020 7371 2121 ✪
Robert Rolls, EC1 020 7606 1166 ✪ M C F
Selfridges, W1 020 7318 3730 ✪
Soho Wine Supply, W1 020 7636 8490
Uncorked, EC2 020 7638 5998
La Vigneronne, SW7 020 7589 6113 ✪
The Vintage House, W1 020 7437 2592

Waterloo Wine, SE1 020 7403 7967
Wilkinson Vintners, N19 020 7272 1982 ✪ M C F
Wimbledon Wine Cellar, SW19 020 8540 9979 ✪
The Wine Cellar, Croydon 020 8657 6936
The Wine Treasury, SW8 020 7793 9999 ✪ M C
The Winery, W9 020 7286 6475 ✪ F

SOUTH EAST

A & A Wines, Cranleigh, Surrey 01483 274666 C
A & B Vintners, Brenchley, Kent 01892 724977 ✪ M C
W. J. Armstrong, East Grinstead, West Sussex 01342 321478
Beaconsfield Wine Cellar, Beaconsfield, Buckinghamshire
   01494 675545
Bentalls, Kingston-upon-Thames, Surrey 020 8546 1001
The Bottleneck, Broadstairs, Kent 01843 861095
F.E. Brown & Son, Hoddesdon, Hertfordshire
   01992 421327 M C
Butlers Wine Cellar, Brighton, East Sussex 01273 698724 ✪
Direct Wines, Windsor 0870 444 8383 M C
Ben Ellis, Brockham, Surrey 01737 842160 ✪ C
English Wine Centre, Alfriston, East Sussex 01323 870164
Eton Vintners, Windsor 01753 790188 M
Le Fleming Wines, Harpenden, Hertfordshire 01582 760125 M C
Four Walls Wine Company, Chilgrove, West Sussex
   01243 535360 ✪ M F
Gallery Wines, Gomshall, Surrey 01483 203795
Garland Wine Cellar, Ashtead, Surrey 01372 275247
General Wine Company, Liphook, Hampshire 01428 727744 ✪

Great Gaddesden Wines, **Harpenden**, Hertfordshire
01582 760606 **M C**

Gunson Fine Wines, South Godstone, Surrey 01342 843974 ✪ **M C**

Hanslope Wines, **Milton Keynes**, Buckinghamshire
01908 510262

The Haslemere Cellar, **Haslemere**, Surrey 01428 645081 ✪

Hedley Wright, **Bishop's Stortford**, Hertfordshire
01279 465818 **C**

Charles Hennings Vintners, **Pulborough**, West Sussex
01798 872485

Just in Case Wine Merchants, **Bishop's Waltham**, Hampshire
01489 892969

David Kibble Wines, **Fontwell**, West Sussex 01243 544111

Laithwaites, **Reading** 0870 444 8282 **M C**

Longford Wines, **Lewes**, East Sussex 01273 400012 **M C**

Milton Sandford Wines, **Knowl Hill**, Berkshire
01628 829449 ✪ **M C**

The Old Forge Wine Cellar, **Storrington**, West Sussex
01903 744246

Portal, Dingwall & Norris, **Emsworth**, Hampshire 01243 377883

Arthur Rackham, **Guildford**, Surrey 01483 722962 **C**

St Martin Vintners, **Brighton**, East Sussex 01273 777788

Turville Valley Wines, **Great Missenden**, Buckinghamshire
01494 868818 ✪ **M C F**

Helen Verdcourt, **Maidenhead**, Berkshire 01628 625577 **M C**

Vin du Van, **Appledore**, Kent 01233 758727 ✪ **M C**

The Vineyard, **Dorking**, Surrey 01306 876828

Vino Vino, **New Malden**, Surrey 07703 436 949 **M C**

Vintage Roots, **Arborfield**, Berkshire 0118 976 1999 **M**

Wine Society, **Stevenage**, Hertfordshire 01438 741177 ✿ M C F
Wycombe Wines, **High Wycombe**, Buckinghamshire
  01494 437228

SOUTH WEST

Arkells Vintners, **Swindon**, Wiltshire 01793 823026
Averys, **Bristol** 0117 921 4146
Beaminster Fine Wines, **Beaminster**, Dorset 01308 862350
Bideford Wines, **Bideford**, Devon 01237 470507
Castang Wine Shippers, **Pelynt**, Cornwall 01503 220359 M C
Clifton Cellars, **Bristol** 0117 973 0287
Brian Coad Fine Wines, **Ivybridge**, Devon 01752 896545 M C
Cochonnet Wines, **Falmouth**, Cornwall 01326 340332
Corks, **Cotham**, Bristol 0117 973 1620
Dartmouth Vintners, **Dartmouth**, Devon 01803 832602
The Dorchester Wine Centre at Eldridge Pope, **Dorchester**, Dorset
  01305 258266 ✿
Draycott Wines, **Topsham**, Devon 01392 874501
Fine Cheese Co., **Bath** 01225 483407
La Forge Wines, **Marksbury**, Bath 01761 472349
Great Western Wine Company, **Bath** 01225 322800
John Harvey & Sons, **Bristol** 0117 927 5006 M C
Richard Harvey Wines, **Wareham**, Dorset 01929 481437 M C
The Jolly Vintner, **Tiverton**, Devon 01884 255644
L & F Jones, **Radstock** near Bath 01761 417117
Laymont & Shaw, **Truro**, Cornwall 01872 270545 M C
The Nobody Inn, **Doddiscombsleigh**, Devon 01647 252394 ✿
Christopher Piper Wines, **Ottery St Mary**, Devon 01404 814139 ✿

Quay West Wines, **Stoke Canon**, Exeter 01392 841833 **C**
R.S. Wines, **Bristol** 0117 963 1780 **M C**
Reid Wines, **Hallatrow**, Bristol 01761 452645 ✪ **M F**
Shaftesbury Fine Wines, **Shaftesbury**, Dorset 01747 850059
Charles Steevenson, **Tavistock**, Devon 01822 616272 **M C**
Totnes Wine Co., **Totnes**, Devon 01803 866357
Trenchermans, **Sherborne**, Dorset 01935 432857
The Vine Trail, **Hotwells**, Bristol 0117 921 1770 ✪ **M C**
Wessex Wines, **Bridport**, Dorset 01308 427177 **C**
Woodhouse Wines, **Blandford**, Dorset 0258 452141
Peter Wylie Fine Wines, **Plymtree**, Devon 01884 277555 ✪ **F**
Yapp Brothers, **Mere**, Wiltshire 01747 860 423 ✪ **M C**

MIDLANDS

Amps Fine Wines of Oundle, **near Peterborough**,
   Northamptonshire 01832 273502
Arnolds, **Broadway**, Worcestershire 01386 852427
Arriba Kettle & Co., **Honeybourne**, Worcestershire
   01386 833024 **C**
Bat & Bottle, **Knightley**, Staffordshire 01785 284495
Bennetts Fine Wines, **Chipping Campden**, Gloucestershire
   01386 840392 ✪
Les Caves du Patron, **Stoneygate**, Leicester 0116 221 8221
Andrew Chapman Fine Wines, **Abingdon**, Oxfordshire
   0845 458 0707
Colombier Vins Fins, **Swadlincote**, Derbyshire
   01283 552552 **M C**
Connollys, **Birmingham** 0121 236 9269

Croque-en-Bouche, **Malvern Wells**, Worcestershire
 01684 565612 ✪ **M C**
Du Vin, **Henley-on-Thames**, Oxfordshire 01491 637888
Evertons, **Ombersley**, Worcestershire 01905 620282
Evingtons Wine Merchants, **Leicester** 0116 254 2702
Gauntleys, **Nottingham** 0115 911 0555
Glumangate Wines, **Chesterfield**, Derbyshire 01246 200499
Patrick Grubb Selections, **Oxford** 01869 340229 ✪
Haynes, Hanson & Clark, **Stow-on-the-Wold**, Gloucestershire
 01451 870808 ✪
Pierre Henck, **Wolverhampton**, West Midlands
 01902 751022 **M C**
George Hill, **Loughborough**, Leicestershire 01509 212717
Hopton Wines, **Kidderminster**, Worcestershire 01299 270734 **M C**
Ian G. Howe, **Newark**, Nottinghamshire 01636 704366
Inspired Wines, **Cleobury Mortimer**, Shropshire 01299 270064
S.H. Jones, **Banbury**, Oxfordshire 01295 251179
Mills Whitcombe, **Lower Maescoed**, Herefordshire
 01873 860222 **C**
Nickolls & Perks, **Stourbridge**, West Midlands 01384 394518
Noble Rot Wine Warehouse, **Bromsgrove**, Worcestershire
 01527 575606
Oxford Wine Company, **Witney**, Oxfordshire 01865 301144 ✪
Thomas Panton, **Tetbury**, Gloucestershire 01666 503088 **M**
Edward Sheldon, **Shipston-on-Stour**, Warwickshire
 01608 661409
Stevens Garnier, **Oxford** 01865 263303
Tanners, **Shrewsbury**, Shropshire 01743 234455 ✪
Waters Wine Merchants, **Coventry**, Warwick 01926 888889

David J. Watt Fine Wines, **Ashby-de-la-Zouch**, Leicestershire
01530 415704 shop, 01530 413953 **M**

Weavers, **Nottingham**, Nottinghamshire 0115 958 0922

Whitebridge Wines, **Stone**, Staffordshire 01785 817229

Whittalls Wines, **Walsall**, West Midlands 01922 636161 **C**

Winchcombe Wine Merchants, **Winchcombe**, Gloucestershire
01242 604313

EASTERN COUNTIES

Adnams Wine Merchants, **Southwold**, Suffolk
01502 727251 ✪

Ameys Wines, **Sudbury**, Suffolk 01787 377144

Bacchanalia, **Cambridge** 01223 576292

Anthony Byrne Fine Wines, **Ramsey**, Cambridgeshire
01487 814555 **M C**

Carley & Webb, **Framlingham**, Suffolk 01728 723503

Peter Graham Wines, **Norwich**, Norfolk 01603 625657

Roger Harris Wines, **Weston Longville**, Norfolk
01603 880171 ✪ **M C**

Richard Kihl, **Aldeburgh**, Suffolk 01728 454455 ✪ **F C**

Lay & Wheeler, **Colchester**, Essex 01206 764446

Luckins Wine Store, **Great Dunmow**, Essex 01371 872839

Oasis Wines, **Southend-on-Sea**, Essex 01702 293999

Thos Peatling, **Bury St Edmunds**, Suffolk 01284 714285

Sandhams Wine Merchants, **Caistor**, Lincolnshire 01472 852118

Seckford Wines, **Woodbridge**, Suffolk 01394 446622 ✪ **M C F**

T & W Wines, **Thetford**, Norfolk 01842 765646

Wines of Interest, **Ipswich**, Suffolk 01473 215752

The Winesmith, Peterborough, Cambridgeshire 01780 783102
Noel Young Wines, Trumpington, Cambridgeshire
   01223 844744 ✪

NORTH WEST

Booths of Stockport, Heaton Moor, Stockport 0161 432 3309
D. Byrne & Co., Clitheroe, Lancashire 01200 423152 ✪
Carringtons, Manchester 0161 881 0099
Cheshire Smokehouse, Wilmslow, Cheshire 01625 540123
Classic Wines, Chester, Cheshire 01244 288444
Corkscrew Wines, Carlisle, Cumbria 01228 543033
deFINE Food and Wine, Sandiway, Cheshire 01606 882101
Rodney Densem Wines, Nantwich, Cheshire 01270 626999
Edencroft Fine Wines, Nantwich, Cheshire 01270 629975
Garrards, Cockermouth, Cumbria 01900 823592
Portland Wine Co., Sale, Manchester 0161 962 8752
Quellyn Roberts, Chester, Cheshire 01244 310455
Scatchard, Liverpool 0151 709 7073
Selfridges, Manchester 0161 629 1234 ✪
Frank Stainton Wines, Kendal, Cumbria 01539 731886
Whitesides, Clitheroe, Lancashire 01200 422281
Willoughbys the Wine Merchants, Manchester 0161 834 6850
WineTime, Milnthorpe, Cumbria 01539 562030 M C

NORTH EAST

Barrels & Bottles, Sheffield 0114 255 6611
Cairns & Hickey, Bramhope, Leeds 0113 267 3746

Chippendale Fine Wines, **Bradford**, West Yorkshire
01274 582424 **M C**

Great Northern Wine Company, **Ripon**, North Yorkshire
01765 606767 **M**

Hoults Wine Merchants, **Huddersfield**, West Yorkshire
01484 510700

House of Townend, **Kingston upon Hull**, East Yorkshire
01482 586582

Michael Jobling, **Newcastle-upon-Tyne** 0191 261 5298 **M C**

John Kelly Wines, **Boston Spa**, West Yorkshire 01937 842965 **M C**

Martinez Fine Wines, **Ilkley**, West Yorkshire 01943 603241 ✪

Mitchells Wine Merchants, **Sheffield** 0114 274 5587

Penistone Court Wine Cellars, **Penistone**, Sheffield
01226 766037 **M C**

Playford Ros, **Thirsk**, North Yorkshire 01845 526777 **M C**

Roberts & Speight, **Beverley**, East Yorkshire 01482 870717

Springfield Wines, **near Huddersfield**, West Yorkshire
01484 864929

Vinceremos, **Leeds** 0113 205 4545 **M C**

The Wright Wine Company, **Skipton**, North Yorkshire
01756 700886 ✪

Wrightson & Co. Wine Merchants, **Darlington** 01325 374134 **M C**

SCOTLAND

Cockburns, **Leith**, Edinburgh 0131 346 1113

Peter Green, **Edinburgh** 0131 229 5925

Inverarity Vaults, **Biggar** 01899 308000

Irvine Robertson, **Edinburgh** 0131 553 3521 **C**

J & H Logan, **Edinburgh** 0131 667 2855
Peckham & Rye, **Glasgow** 0141 445 4555 ✪
Raeburn Fine Wines, **Edinburgh** 0131 554 2652 ✪
Laurence Smith, **Edinburgh** 0131 667 3327 **M C**
Valvona & Crolla, **Edinburgh** 0131 556 6066 ✪
Villeneuve Wines, **Peebles**, **Haddington** and **Edinburgh**
   01721 722500 ✪

WALES

Ballantynes, **Cowbridge**, Vale of Glamorgan 01446 774840 ✪
Irma Fingal-Rock, **Monmouth**, Monmouthshire 01600 712372
Joseph Keegan, **Holyhead**, Isle of Anglesey 01407 762333
Terry Platt Wine Merchants, **Llandudno**, Conwy
   01492 874099 ✪ **M C**
Shaws, **Beaumaris**, Isle of Anglesey 01248 810328
William Stedman, **Caerleon**, Newport 01633 430055
James Williams, **Narberth**, Pembrokeshire 01834 862200

NORTHERN IRELAND

Direct Wine Shipments, **Belfast**, Northern Ireland 028 9050 8000 ✪
James Nicholson, **Crossgar**, Co. Down, Northern Ireland
   028 4483 0091 ✪

CHANNEL ISLANDS

Bergerac Wine Cellar, **St Helier**, Jersey 01534 870756
Dunnells Ltd, **St Peter Port**, Guernsey 01534 736418

Victor Hugo Wines, **St Saviour**, Jersey 01534 507977
The Sommelier Wine Co., **St Peter Port**, Guernsey
  01481 721677 ✪

If you are a wine merchant in the UK and would like to be
mentioned on this list, or if your details are listed incorrectly,
the author and publisher will be happy to amend later editions.
   We have tried to make **The Wine List** as helpful as possible
but if you have any ideas as to how we could improve it then write
to The Wine List, c/o Headline Book Publishing, 338 Euston Road,
London, NW1 3BH.

TABLE OF ABBREVIATIONS

Asd	Asda
Boo	E.H. Booth & Co.
Bot	Bottoms Up
Coo	Co-operative Group (CWS)
M&S	Marks & Spencer
Mor	Wm Morrison
Odd	Oddbins
OFW	Oddbins Fine Wine
Saf	Safeway